G000139922

Volume 34   Number 3   Autumn 2010

Foreword

It gives me great pleasure to write the foreword to this edition of *Adoption & Fostering* marking BAAF's 30th anniversary.

When I was a judge in the family division, I was required to make decisions in complex situations and to consider many different points of view. These include not only those of the local authority, birth parents and children, but also complicated medical and forensic assessments and research findings on child development. Thus, in facilitating the development of substitute care, whether fostering or adoption, a multi-professional perspective is essential. One of BAAF's great achievements is to have encouraged this and sought the highest standards in its training, publications and specialist legal, health, black perspectives and research groups. It has gained the respect of all the professions involved in the care of children.

Many of the decisions that have to be made concern long-term outcomes for children, and there is an inevitable tension between those which have to be taken now and estimates of their likely effect in future years. Again, through its research, publications and dissemination activities, BAAF has strived to ensure that the best evidence is available to a wide audience. In disseminating research findings, BAAF has always been strictly non-partisan, committed to the welfare of children rather than to doctrinaire policies or specific interest groups. When it has been felt necessary, it has challenged current thinking and policies, as illustrated in Tony Hall and colleagues' article describing the arguments surrounding transracial placements in the 1980s.

BAAF has made great efforts to link different sources of information, the nature of which often makes them difficult to reconcile. There are abstractions in the law, with concepts such as the welfare principle or significant harm; there are the complexities of research studies, rarely providing unequivocal findings; and then there are the difficulties of practice – a mixture of art and science, as outlined in John Triseliotis's article on contact. BAAF's efforts to marry all of these are manifest in its publications, which range from erudite reports, to practice manuals and sensitively drafted information for children and families. Very few other voluntary organisations produce such a range of materials.

BAAF has always been quick to face new challenges. Some examples over the years include: open adoption; the requirement to practice from human rights legislation; controversy surrounding intercountry adoption and transracial placements; dealing with revelations of past abuse in care; the growth of independent care agencies; adopted people's access to birth records; supporting gay and lesbian carers; developments in AID, DNA and genetic screening; independent representation of birth parents and children; the need to develop methods to ascertain children's wishes; and the need to move from a system to an outcome focus. These responses again comprise a range of activities – publications, training, media pronouncements and submitting evidence to committees and official inquiries.

But there is no room for complacency. There are many areas where knowledge is still insufficient to be confident about the decisions made. The outcome evidence on different types of placement is still weak, changing behaviour remains difficult, methods of supporting carers and care leavers are still tentative, and unvalidated ideas can be given undue publicity. The current political climate will be less sympathetic to costly projects, administrative systems are under review and privatisation and devolution are likely to produce a plethora of new agencies and approaches.

But BAAF has never been afraid of change and I remain confident that it will continue to play a key role in promoting children's welfare, whatever challenges lie ahead.

The Right Hon. Baroness Elizabeth Butler-Sloss GBE
BAAF Patron

Change and continuity 1980–2010

Roy Parker considers key developments in services for children separated from their birth families in England and Wales over the last 30 years.

Roy Parker is
Emeritus Professor
of Social Policy,
University of Bristol

Key words: children
in care, children's
services, 1980–2010

Introduction and a little background

In the year that BAAF was founded (1980), the National Children's Bureau (NCB) in London published the report of a working party that it had convened to consider the care of separated children (Parker, 1980). This publication is helpful in appreciating the changes in policy, practice and problems that have occurred over BAAF's 30-year history.

The report reflected a longstanding concern about the nature and extent of appropriate state involvement in parenting children, a relationship that became particularly manifest in the Second World War when well over a million children, unaccompanied by their mothers, were evacuated from cities and coastal resorts to safer areas (see, Titmuss, 1950).[1] This upheaval revealed two things. First, that a worrying minority of the children, especially from the cities, arrived in a poor state of well-being and behaved in ways that were regarded as reflecting a disturbed upbringing. Secondly, enough of the children demonstrated distress at their separation to cause concern. How these two revelations related to each other was difficult to determine; but separately and together they raised questions about how children were to be better cared for, particularly those who were separated from their families.[2] This disquiet was further accentuated by, for example, the death of Dennis O'Neill who died from abuse in his foster home in 1945 (Monckton, 1945), by the findings of the Curtis and Clyde committees that were issued in 1946 and by a variety of pamphlets, such as that produced by the New Education Fellowship entitled *Children in Wartime*.

In a way, however, the concerns that were generated in this period subsided once the reforms inaugurated under the 1948 Children Act (see, Parker, 1983; Cretney, 1998) had overcome at least some of the problems associated with the separated child. Then, in 1963,[3] local authorities were at last permitted to spend money on preventing children from coming into care and that too seemed to be an important step forward. However, the death of Maria Colwell in 1973 (Secretary of State for Social Services, 1974) revived a variety of concerns about both policy and practice, with the press bringing the tragedy into a new public prominence (see, Parton, 1985).

In the social sciences, interest in the effects of separation on children's development was also growing. John Bowlby (1951) had highlighted the separation of a child from his or her mother as a risk factor for poor social and psychological adjustment, although by the time of the NCB report this rather rigid view had been tempered by other researchers, particularly Michael Rutter (1972), who argued that the effects depended upon the circumstances under which the child

---

[1] Titmuss (1950) provides an excellent account of evacuation in the main text, but the detailed statistics are to be found in the appendices. Together with the unaccompanied children there were those who went with their mothers under the government scheme; but as well as these a 'very large' but unknown number of evacuations were arranged privately.

[2] See, for example, Burlingham and Freud (1942), Isaacs (1941), Women's Group on Social Welfare (1948) and, later, Holman (1995).

[3] Section 1 of the 1963 Children Act required local authorities 'to make available such advice, guidance and assistance as may promote the welfare of children by diminishing the need to receive children into or keep them in care . . .'

was separated as well as what happened next.

Although the NCB initiative occurred at the end of a decade that had seen several important reforms, such as the creation of integrated social services departments, the 1975 Act[4] and the closure of residential nurseries for young children, many earlier concerns and dilemmas persisted. For example, institutional placements continued to be widely employed, the number of children in care had risen alarmingly and the balance of risk between endeavouring to keep children in their families and removing them for their protection remained a disputed issue, as did the associated question of the appropriate role of the state and therefore when and how it should or could assume parent-like responsibilities.

In its 1980 report, the NCB working party endeavoured to address some of these issues, to present the facts and to suggest possible ways forward. Yet reliable facts were rather thin on the ground. There was a dearth of robust research evidence, not just about the effects of separation on different children but also concerning the long-term experiences of children in care or at risk but left at home. Indeed, although in 1967 the NCB (then the National Bureau for Co-operation in Child Care) had published extensive reviews of research on adoption (Pringle et al, 1967), residential care (Dinnage and Pringle, 1967a) and foster care (Dinnage and Pringle, 1967b), many of the studies that were reported were small scale, unscientific or from overseas, particularly from

the US. For example, it could list only three ongoing projects in the UK concerned with foster care. Nevertheless, the 1970s did see more studies of a number of aspects of child care, most notably that of Jane Rowe and Lydia Lambert's *Children who Wait*, published in 1973. Throughout the 1970s, further material began to be available (for example, Triseliotis, 1973; Millham *et al*, 1978), but even by 1980 glaring gaps remained in what we knew about the many issues that surrounded the children's services and the children and families whom they served. Many case histories, commentaries and theories were offered, but most had not been tested empirically (see, Axford *et al*, 2005).

So, what have been the main changes since BAAF's foundation in 1980 and how might they be explained?

Statistics

One way of approaching the identification of significant changes in child care during the last 30 years is to look at the available statistics. There are two reasons for doing so. First, they show changes in the 'profile' of the child care population and secondly, what is recorded (and under what headings) sheds light on the issues that gain prominence. Here are a few statistical reference points.[5]

The decline in the number of children in care is perhaps the most striking shift, from 100,700 in 1978 to 65,600 in 2009. That is a fall of 35 per cent. Although significant, what does it reflect? The answer may be different if we try to

---

[4] See National Foster Care Association, *A Review of the Children Act [1975] 10 Years On* (1986). The Act encouraged the adoption of children in care by, for example, requiring local authorities to act as adoption agencies and by introducing the concept of 'freeing for adoption'. It also aimed to give carers greater security, for instance by the creation of custodianship orders for which foster parents could apply, although few did. The critics focused upon the potential reduction of parental rights.

[5] Unless otherwise indicated, the statistics are for England and Wales although now, unlike 1980 and earlier, they are no longer published together and therefore may vary in format or appear at different times. The reader will notice that for the start of the period under consideration the figures are often for 1978. This is because the NCB report, which has been used as something of a starting point, although published in 1980, employed mainly figures from 1978. The source throughout is *Children Looked After in England (and Wales)*, now published by the Department of Education but earlier by the DCSF and DHSS (latest: www.dcsf.gov.uk/rsgateway/DB/SFR/).

explain the large number in 1978 or if we concentrate on the reasons for the subsequent decline.

The number of children in care had begun to rise in the early 1970s but had reached a plateau in the years 1977–80. The increase was partly due to the inclusion of the approved schools (institutions mainly for young offenders) population at the beginning of 1971, roughly an extra 10,000; but 'the rediscovery of abuse' in that decade may also have been a factor as more children at risk were identified. Certainly, there was a surge in referrals from many quarters. The reduction in the number in care is probably easier to explain: essentially a shift in focus towards prevention, together with a transfer of attention and resources to 'family and community work' and, after the Children Act 1989, the fact that young offenders and those failing to go to school could no longer be committed to care by the courts.

Both the proportion and the number of children in foster homes have witnessed a dramatic growth since 1980. The proportion rose from 35 per cent to 73 per cent in 2009 and the number by about 13,000, despite concerns about 'hard-to-place' children (see Triseliotis, 1980; Hill, 1999). The change was driven by the quest to reduce reliance on residential care but also, early on, by a remarkable increase in the number of children committed to care by the courts being allowed home 'on trial'. This group was counted in the foster care total of which, in 1978, it accounted for 19 per cent. It reached almost 25 per cent a few years later (see, Farmer and Parker, 1991). It is now recorded separately as 'placement with parents'. Thus, although it helped to boost the recorded number in foster care in the 1980s it ceased to do so soon afterwards: the growth in foster care could no longer be attributed to this oddity of statistical classification. A mixture of other factors has to be considered. It may be that a wider pool of foster carers began to be tapped; that more marginal foster parents were being used; that better payments had an effect, together with

more determined foster family finding, to which BAAF has made an evident contribution. In addition, there were fewer residential places available as an alternative. Indeed, whereas 37 per cent of children in care in 1978 were in some form of residential accommodation, this proportion now stands at eleven per cent in England and at four per cent in Wales.

One other notable change in the intervening years has been in adoption from care. In 1978 these adoptions numbered 1,600 (2% of all discharges) but they had risen to 3,560 by 2009 (5% of those leaving care). But the age of those adopted has also altered. In 1978, 23 per cent were under one year of age but by 2009 only two per cent. In part, this reflected the virtual disappearance of the stigma associated with illegitimacy and thus to fewer unmarried mothers relinquishing their babies for adoption. But from the late 1990s onwards adoption from care also received considerable encouragement from central government. With all of this came a marked shift away from adoption being regarded as meeting the needs of infertile couples to it being seen as a way of meeting the needs of certain children for a permanent home. One other change has been the decline in the role of voluntary adoption organisations, partly because local authorities are now required to act as adoption agencies themselves and therefore call less often upon the help of the voluntary sector. This is reflected in BAAF's current membership, which now stands at 211 local authorities and 32 voluntary societies (15%) compared with 126 and 49 (39%) in 1980.

Legal changes have also modified the in-care 'profile' considerably. For example, as we have seen, since the 1989 Children Act children are no longer committed to care as offenders; in 1978 they comprised 18,000 of the total, or 18 per cent. Likewise, children are no longer admitted for 'non-school attendance'; but in 1978 there were 4,500 in care for this reason, or some five per cent. These exclusions help to explain declining numbers in care, but they also reflect changed attitudes towards the treatment of these problems as well as the re-classification of 'reasons for being in care'. Some who fell into these former groups will now fall into the category of being in care because of their 'neglect or abuse'. This designation now covers 61 per cent of the children in care, up from 21 per cent in 1978.

It should also be borne in mind that the 1989 Act required more exacting conditions to be met before a court could issue an order committing a child to local authority care (see, *Journal of Children's Services*, 2010). Indeed, the shift that the Act represented towards the better protection of parents' rights and towards the assumption that a child should remain at home unless 'significant harm' was established may well have contributed to the reduction of the number 'looked after'. However, whereas in 1978 45 per cent of children in care in England were subject to care orders, by 2009 this had risen to 58 per cent, although the actual number had fallen from 45,500 to 38,000.

The much closer attention being paid over the last decade or so to the problems of neglect and abuse is, of course, a notable change since 1980, even though we cannot be sure whether there has been a real increase in the phenomenon or whether there is now more awareness. Nonetheless, as we have seen, the growth in its salience is reflected in the statistics. It now dominates the scene in most children's services as well as in the media, and although there was concern in 1980, it did not occupy such a central position, despite the disquiet about child abuse that had begun to grow in the 1970s. What we have seen in recent years is an intensification of the tension between striving to keep child and family together (or achieving their reunification) and the need to protect children from actual or potential harm through their removal into care. This has caused fluctuations in the politics of child welfare.

The emergence of 'new' issues tends to be signalled by the assembly of new statistics. For example, in 1978 there were none on the ethnicity or education of children in care. The 2009 returns cover both issues. They tell us that 27 per cent of the in-care population in England were classified as not 'white British' (a considerable over-representation) and we now know the educational attainments of children in care at Years 2, 6, 9 and 11 as well as the gap between their achievements and other children. Other new statistics have also made an appearance; for example, the number of young mothers of 12 years old or over who are in care (330 in England, of whom 280 were 16 or 17) and information on 'outcome indicators', again reflecting a considerable change since 1980 when little attention was paid to the assessment and measurement of outcomes. Such changes in what is enumerated do mirror the rise and fall of the issues of the day, but because of this, data are liable to be discontinuous, making comparisons over time that much more difficult. There is also the problem of obtaining an overall picture of the situation in the UK as each constituent country publishes its own statistics that, in their turn, reflect different policy and legal situations. In this respect, the reader should be reminded that the figures provided in this article refer to England and Wales. Both Scotland and Northern Ireland warrant a similar review.

Changes in politics, policies and practice

There have been, of course, major transformations in the social and economic structure of the country since 1980. Some of the repercussions will have affected children's services, although it is not clear which, to what extent, or how. There has been the increase in divorce, the growth in the number of step-parent families, more one-parent families, youth unemployment, growing inequality, more asylum seekers (3,700 of them in care in England in 2009, but none listed in 1980) – and so the list might be continued. However, apart from such changes there have been other important alterations in the 'climate' in which these services have operated. Let us consider some of them.

By 1980 there had been a discernable increase in what might be regarded as pressure group activity. For example, the Family Rights Group had been set up in 1974; the National Association for Young People in Care a year later, and the Children's Legal Centre in 1981. Other new groups followed. Associated journals began to make an appearance, such as the *Who Cares?* magazine in 1985. The rights issue continued to gain in significance, both for children and for their parents (including fathers) as well as for carers, much of it exemplified by the Children Act 1989. Inquiries into the deaths of children in care or of children for whom social services carried some responsibility proliferated. Criticism abounded, much of it heightened by a more robust media. In 1983, the House of Commons Social Services Committee (1984) chose to inquire into the state of the child care services and published its telling report a year later. In 2003, a Children's Commissioner (Ombudsman) was appointed, partly in response to the report of the inquiry into abuses in children's homes in North Wales (Waterhouse, 2000), but also in response to pressure from several groups concerned with children's rights. Such developments have meant that children's services have become exposed to much closer scrutiny and to influences that pull them in many directions. The work becomes more complicated and demanding. Expectations are raised and calls increase for government to respond to each new disquieting event, and often more rapidly than before. 'Remedial' policies emerge, making it hard for practitioners to keep up.

In the last 30 years research has come to play a more important part in both policy and practice. Of course, in many ways Rowe and Lambert set the ball rolling in 1973 but the establishment of the National Children's Bureau two years later was also significant, as was the decision of the Department of Health to sponsor a programme of research into children's services. BAAF, too, increased its encouragement of research and became an important outlet for the publication of its results. Although the influence of research has waxed and waned, there is certainly much more of it: its findings appear in a growing number of journals; material is to be found on the internet, and organisations like Research in Practice and Making Research Count seek to make studies available to practitioners. In short, we have had a proliferation of information since 1980. The challenge now becomes how best to use and manage it, not least because it is not all of the same quality and, in any case, is capable of introducing new doubts and uncertainties as well as valuable illumination.

One should also consider how policies have changed over the last 30 years. There are several difficulties in doing this. One arises from the fact that each local authority exercises a measure of discretion about what it does, even though the edicts of central government impose certain constraints. Moreover, policies that are established by administrations do not always filter down to the field and, even when they do, they may fail to be fully or consistently implemented; and some 'policies' emerge from the growing regularity of what is done without necessarily having been introduced by a superordinate authority.

Furthermore, when considering the changes in policies that have affected children's services since 1980, it is necessary to cast the net fairly widely because what happens in other fields can have an effect on both the demand for them and their supply. There is, as Jean Packman put it, 'a tangle of services which [lies] beyond the public child care system whose activities are clearly related to it' (1986, p 7). Shifts in the policies adopted with respect to welfare payments, housing, education, health and the justice system all have the potential to affect children's services, as do those pursued by the voluntary and private service sectors: take, for example, the rise in private foster family-finding agencies or the growing official encouragement for the public sector to utilise the services of voluntary organisations.

Some policies have come and gone and some have cancelled each other out. So, what might one select as significant? I would choose four, but others could be added. First, there has been the growing emphasis upon 'prevention'; that is, upon the general duty of local authorities 'to promote the welfare of children by diminishing the need for them to be received into care, to be kept in care, or to be brought to court' which was re-codified in the Child Care Act of 1980. That intention has remained intact and, especially during the last 20 years or so, has been supported by the expansion of services devoted to day care for pre-school children and to family support.

The second policy development that I would include would be the greater attention being paid to children's wishes and feelings and to what they have to say about their experiences. This, of course, is related to the rights of the child that have been increasingly incorporated in legislative requirements, not least in the Children Act 1989. Even though difficulties remain, not least when it comes to young children and in moving from what individual children tell us to generalising for the many, the very fact of consultation marks a laudable and important break with the past.

Many additional requirements for the collection of both individual and aggregate data have been imposed since 1980; this would be the third policy development that I would select and echoes what has been said earlier. Now, for example, there is the children in need census to be provided and the seven national indicators to be assembled (for instance, on children's emotional behaviour). More emphasis has been placed on timely reviews and upon the formulation and recording of plans, particularly in child protection cases. Such developments provide important details about the performance of individual authorities; but it is difficult to know exactly what difference they have made to what is done and to what is achieved by social workers grappling with the problems of individual children. What is clear is that as a result of these requirements (and the growth of research), both administrators and social workers have much more information available to them than they would have had in 1980, although, as we have said, it may be difficult for them to sift out, or even to find, what is relevant for their particular purpose.

A fourth important and related policy development has been the increasing emphasis placed upon outcomes and their evaluation, and upon targets of various kinds, partly driven by anxieties about levels of expenditure. In 2008, for example, the gross cost of children looked after in England was £2.2 billion, up from £1.3 billion in 2000; that is a rise of about 40 per cent. In 1978, the cost of care stood at £190 million. Likewise, in 1978 the average weekly cost per child in care was £48 while in 2000 it was £430 and by 2009 it had reached £707 or £36,770 a year. Although it is difficult to make accurate comparisons, expenditure on these services has risen in real terms – hence the preoccupation with getting 'value for money'. More questions now arise about what differences these increases have made; for example, the doubling of expenditure on fostering between 2000 and 2008.

With regard to practice, it is difficult to know which aspects of the system have improved or deteriorated, although more staff are now trained than 30 years ago. There is certainly a broader range of perspectives and theoretical developments; for example, those that address issues of attachment, child development and trauma. Even so, it is hard to see much application of theory in most of the work that has to be done in children's services. It may be that this would change were the tempo of that work to be reduced and if the connection between theory and practice became more evident in more cases.

Yet it could be that wider social forces have offset some of the gains that might have been expected of better social work practice. Likewise, it is difficult to judge whether the in-care experience of children is more satisfactory than it was and, if so, to what that is attributable. Certainly, much has been done with that end in mind. For example, children appear to change their placements less often, but some of this improvement could be due to the closure of observation and assessment centres which, in 1980, accounted for 21 per cent of all first placements and from which residents moved on after a short stay. However, the emphasis on 'permanence' that gained ground during the 1990s may well have helped to reduced the frequency of disruptions, as could the greater support offered to foster parents.

Of course, the issues surrounding children in care are inextricably linked to the social work that is being done (or that needs to be done) with families in order to prevent that eventuality or to achieve restoration. The scale and nature of these latter activities are more difficult to chart, whether it be in terms of their duration, intensity, effectiveness or cost. But to the extent that such work has expanded (and there is every sign that it has), that devoted to the child in care may have suffered somewhat. Indeed, the question of how scarce social work and other resources can be best deployed seems to have become more pressing (not least because of the emphasis upon evaluation) and although the answers are liable to be affected by each new crisis or exposure, the issue remains as taxing as it did in 1980. And that leads me to my last observation.

What has remained largely unchanged?

Although we have developed new ideas and theories about what should be done to promote the welfare of vulnerable children, core issues remain. They concern principally the deleterious effects of significantly poor parenting and the related disruptions to children's lives. Of course, the scale of the problem remains a matter of dispute but not its seriousness for the children affected. There is a common assumption that we understand better than we did the reasons for these devastating upheavals: poverty, poor parenting, marital conflict, alcohol, drugs, run-down estates, the absence of fathers, and so the list continues. But, in fact, the passage of 30 years has offered us little by way of an understanding that would give clear guidance about what best to do structurally: that is, across the board. What understanding we possess is most convincing at a case-by-case level.

On a more administrative level, certain other things have shown little change either; for example, the ratio of boys to girls in care (3 to 2), the problems surrounding the co-ordination of different services (despite much exhortation to do better), the amount of discretion that is able to be exercised by frontline staff, or the important influence that the courts and other related services have on what is and can be done in child care.

Despite considerable efforts and specific legislation such as the Children (Leaving Care) Act of 2000, children who leave care at 18 still face much the same daunting prospect now as they did in 1980, although there are few figures for that year. In 2009, however, the largest proportion (43%) of 19-year-olds who had been in care in England – at least since they were 16 – were classified as being in 'independent living' while the next highest proportion (13%) were living with parents or relatives. Six per cent had been lost to view and three per cent were in custody. On a different analysis, one finds that 31 per cent were not in training or employment, but five per cent fell into that category because they were ill or disabled.

Although its scale has been reduced, there remains the problem of 'disruption'; that is, of a child having a sequence of placements. During 2009, 10.7 per cent of children in care in England had had three or more placements. Hence, there is an enduring concern about stability and not just in respect to children's placements. There continues to be considerable turnover of staff, especially in certain areas, often associated with a persistence of unfilled posts, both of which are likely to have a deleterious effect upon the quality of services. And that leads to one other continuity.

In 1980, there were marked differences on many matters between the local authorities responsible for the provision of children's services. For instance, in 1978 the number of children in care per 1,000 of the population under 18 ranged from 27.2 in Tower Hamlets to 3.6 in Surrey and the percentage in foster care from 70 in Warwickshire to 24 in Greenwich. Similar differences exist today. In England, in 2009, the in-care rates stretched from 14.6 in Manchester to 2.0 in Wokingham and although the highs and lows cluster around the same kinds of areas, the upper levels are coming down; for instance, Tower Hamlets falling to 7.1. Similarly, although the rate of foster care has increased, differences still exist: rates now spread from 89 per cent in Hartlepool to 61 per cent in Salford. Indeed, although the pattern may have changed in some respects there continue to be substantial differences between the problems that authorities face. To take one further example: in 2009 just three authorities (Croydon, Kent and Hillingdon) looked after almost 30 per cent of all unaccompanied asylum-seeking children.

I hazard a guess that one other thing that has changed little since 1980 is the public perception of children's services. Considerable opprobrium continues to be heaped upon social workers and upon those with whom they work. In terms of the politics of these services, this is a significant problem and one that may intensify in the atmosphere of 'welfare cuts'. The image of children's services has to be improved as well as their quality.

References

Axford N, Berry V, Little M and Morpeth L, *Forty Years of Research, Policy and Practice in Children's Services*, Chichester: John Wiley & Sons, 2005

Bowlby J, *Maternal Care and Mental Health*, Geneva: WHO, 1951

Burlingham D and Freud A, *Young Children in War-time in a Residential War Nursery*, London: Allen & Unwin, 1942

Clyde (Chair), *Report of the Committee on Homeless Children*, cmd 6911, Edinburgh: HMSO, 1946

Cretney S, 'The state as parent: the Children Act 1948 in retrospect', *Law Quarterly Review* 114, pp 419–59, July 1998

Curtis (Chair), *Report of the Care of Children Committee*, cmd 6922, London: HMSO, 1946

Dinnage R and Pringle M, *Residential Care: Facts and fallacies*, London: Longmans, 1967a

Dinnage R and Pringle M, *Foster Home Care: Facts and fallacies*, London: Longmans, 1967b

Farmer E and Parker R, *Trials and Tribulations*, London: HMSO, 1991

Hill M (ed), *Signposts in Fostering*, London: BAAF, 1999

Holman R, *The Evacuation*, Oxford: Lion, 1995

House of Commons Social Services Committee, *Report: Children in Care*, HC 380, 1984

Isaacs S (ed), *The Cambridge Evacuation Survey*, London: Methuen, 1941

Journal of Children's Services 5:2, Special issue on the Children Act 1989, 2010

Millham S, Bullock R and Hosie K, *Locking up Children*, Farnborough: Saxon House, 1978

Monckton (Chair), *Report on the Circumstances that led to the Boarding-out of Dennis and Terence O'Neill at Bank Farm, Minsterly, and the Steps taken to Supervise their Welfare*, London: HMSO, 1945

New Education Fellowship, *Children in Wartime*, London: New Education Fellowship, circa 1946

National Foster Care Association, *A Review of the Children Act [1975] 10 Years On*, London: NFCA, 1986

Packman J, *Who Needs Care?*, Oxford: Blackwell, 1986

Parker R (ed), *Caring for Separated Children*, London: Macmillan, 1980

Parker R, 'The gestation of reform: the Children Act 1948', in Bean P and MacPherson S (eds), *Approaches to Welfare*, London: Routledge & Kegan Paul, 1983

Parton N, *The Politics of Child Abuse*, London: Macmillan, 1985

Pringle M, with Dewdney M, Crellin E and

Dinnage R, *Adoption: Facts and fallacies*, London: Longmans, 1967

Rowe J and Lambert L, *Children who Wait*, London: ABAA, 1973

Rutter M, *Maternal Deprivation Re-assessed*, Harmondsworth: Penguin, 1972

Secretary of State for the Social Services, *Report of the Committee of Inquiry into the Care and Supervision Provided in Relation to Maria Colwell*, London: HMSO, 1974

Titmuss R, *Problems of Social Policy*, London: HMSO, 1950

Triseliotis J, *In Search of Origins*, London: Routledge & Kegan Paul, 1973

Triseliotis J (ed), *New Developments in Foster Care and Adoption*, London: Routledge & Kegan Paul,1980

Waterhouse (Chair), *Lost in Care: Report of the Tribunal of Inquiry into the Abuse of Children in the Care of the former county councils of Gwyndd and Clwyd since 1974*, London: Department of Health, 2000

Women's Group on Social Welfare, *The Neglected Child and His Family*, London: Oxford University Press, 1948

The changing context of child and family social work

Child and family social work has changed considerably over the past 60 years. **Arabella Weyts** and **John Randall** chart these developments in England since the radical legislation of 1948 and identify enduring tensions that arise from role conflicts, shared responsibilities and balancing specialist and generalist work, each of which presents challenges for overarching organisations such as BAAF.

Arabella Weyts is a Pedagogical Researcher and Practitioner in Ghent, Belgium

John Randall is Post-adoption Social Worker, Families for Children, Devon

Key words: child and family social work, history

Introduction

Although the welfare aims of child and family social work have been consistent over the years, the activities and arrangements for achieving these aims have continually changed. For instance, there were at least four major reforms in the five decades after the end of the Second World War. These were significant for BAAF because it is through practitioners that the organisation's ideas are implemented and refined.

The first significant development was the introduction of training courses for professional child care officers (as opposed to the general welfare workers and boarding out officers who had serviced the old Poor Law system), recommended in the interim report of the Curtis Committee (1945), which had been set up by the UK Government to inquire into the care of children. This meant that a group of newly trained professionals was available for the new local authority children's departments when they were eventually set up in 1948, thus implementing the recommendations of the Committee's final report (Curtis, 1946). However, by the 1960s it had become clear that the role and focus of the work of these child care officers were too limited. Children often lived in families who faced multiple difficulties, such as turbulent adult relationships, parental illness and disability, all of which required responses from different professionals. The child care officer's narrow focus on children, although important, was proving restrictive, with too many professionals from too many agencies being involved with the same people. At the same time, a new development with an emphasis on preventive work, as opposed to managing the admission and discharge of children from care, was beginning to emerge, supported by the Children Act 1963, which permitted expenditure on prevention, thus giving a mandate to virtually unlimited activity although resources remained scarce.

All of these trends suggested the benefits of a third development: a family service delivered by one agency. This approach was endorsed by the Seebohm Committee, which reviewed local authority and allied personal social services and reported in 1968 (Seebohm, 1968). The result was the amalgamation into a new social services department (SSD) of the local authority children's welfare, parts of local health provision and mental health services, all of which had assumed responsibility for the welfare of families following the abolition of the Poor Law after the Second World War. The Seebohm Report saw the new SSDs as community and family oriented, with a preventive outlook. The whole approach – at the level of departmental responsibility – was meant to be generic, giving individual social workers the chance to work across traditional divisions of children, adults, disabilities and mental health, depending on the needs of the case. However, generic responsibility did not necessarily mean generic caseloads or generic teams but a more co-ordinated approach. Thus, social workers remained for the most part specialists, with qualified social workers concentrating on mental health and child care cases, and social work assistants and less qualified workers focusing on what were assumed to be less complicated referrals, such as the elderly and the disabled (Parsloe and Stevenson, 1978).

In addition to this broad mandate, SSDs had also taken on further responsibilities for the approved (reform) school population of young offenders and the community care of the sick and elderly – an increase in the range of work that necessitated more training and more qualified staff. The increase in size and remit was such that Challis (1990) could characterise SSDs in the early 1980s as being too large, too impersonal, overly bureaucratic, out of touch and unresponsive to people's needs.

A key question in this discussion was how this new combination of skills, falling under the generic title of social work, related to other personal social services, whether in the type of social care offered or the division of responsibility among voluntary organisations, families' own resources and community provision. If social workers were to provide the traditional individual casework undertaken by child care officers, which not all users of personal social services require, what should be their relationship with other service providers, such as residential or day care staff and foster carers? In effect, social workers came to dominate the area offices and managed a substantial part of the referral system, but other services, such as management, administration and training, often remained separate with different interests and independence to define their own role (Challis, 1990). It was not surprising, therefore, that around the time BAAF was inaugurated in the early 1980s, the government-sponsored but independent Barclay Committee was set up to review the roles and tasks of social workers and consider issues such as size, bureaucracy and relationships between professionals and users.

While the Committee's report (Barclay, 1982) did not result in legislation, it clarified the tasks of social workers within social work departments and highlighted their pivotal role, so initiating a fourth development. The social work task was viewed as 'social care planning', which meant identifying sources of help and incorporating them into an overall plan for individuals and families. Counselling was central to all this activity, whether the task was assessment or therapy. At the same time, the report emphasised that social workers did not have the monopoly of concern or solutions (p 35). Their main contribution was to develop a model of community social work, recognising the contribution of individual casework but promoting the creation and mobilisation of resources in the community and the early identification of need. However, the question remained: Should social workers be 'gatekeepers' to all personal social services as managers of the 'social care plan' or should they merely be one of several specialist workers? While there was general agreement about the role of social workers, not all of the Committee members could agree on the best ways of organising the profession.

These tensions were confirmed by Bar-On (1990) who, as an overseas observer found that, although social workers described their task as one of 'people changing' or treatment in its broadest sense, their time was mostly spent on 'people processing'. This contrast between social workers' perceptions of their work (echoed by those who trained them) and the 'broker role' that many actually played had implications for practice. In the latter situation, the power relationship between professional and client was more equal, the goals sought more specific and the interaction more reciprocal – interestingly, the very qualities that families said they wanted from professionals.

These discussions about social work were further complicated by the difficulties of defining precisely who constitutes a 'social worker'. Much of the published evidence on professional activity focused on social work as delivered by SSDs rather than by the profession per se, and a number of qualified individuals did not see their activity and effectiveness adequately represented in this definition. Examples were those in youth offending teams, psychiatric settings, residential units or projects managed by voluntary or independent organisations. It is, therefore, important to stress that the focus of this article is primarily on social workers in statutory social/children's services departments, the vast majority of whom have a professional qualification.

The work of children's departments 1948–1970

In order to explore the historical antecedents of current practice, it is helpful to look at the empirical evidence about work with children and families after the implementation of the Children Act 1948. Two sources of information – John Stroud's (1965) *An Introduction to the Child Care Service* and Grey's (1969) Home Office Report, *Workloads in Children's Departments* – are helpful in this respect.

Stroud lists the duties of a child care officer and identifies 18 areas of work. Important for understanding the changing roles of social workers is the fact that many of these tasks have remained constant while others have disappeared or been replaced. It is interesting that even then, the emphasis was on general supervisory tasks rather than a specific activity to solve an identified problem and with a stress on working with groups rather than individuals. His list is as follows:

1. supervising and helping families where children are 'at risk';

2. investigating parents' applications for their children to enter care;

3. working with parents of children in care to help reunification;

4. identifying foster homes, assessing applicants and matching children with placement;

5. supervising foster children boarded out by the local authority;

6. supervising foster children placed under private arrangements by their own parents;

7. visiting children in homes, schools, hospitals, hostels and residential employment;

8. supervising and befriending adolescents who have been in care;

9. assessing prospective adopters and helping to place a suitable child;

10. supervising children placed for adoption;

11. acting as guardian ad litem for children about to be adopted;

12. representing the local authority in the juvenile courts;

13. making inquiries for other local authorities or families;

14. keeping statutory written records;

15. helping with the practical training of students;

16. assisting the local authority's work as an adoption agency;

17. assessing parental income and arranging for contributions;

18. aftercare of children released from approved schools.

Stroud saw family casework as the fundamental task of a child care officer and defined this as, 'the way in which one person helps another, through a relationship based on mutual respect and made effective because professional knowledge of human affairs, and professional skill in making them comprehensible, help the client towards solving his own problems' (Stroud, 1965).

In *Away from Home: A history of child care*, Parker (1990) summarises child care before 1948 as the era when practice was dominated by 'severance': removing children from harmful parents, severing links between the two and actively or passively discouraging their reconciliation. What is striking in the Stroud list is the evidence by 1965 of a move away from a total preoccupation with managing separated children. Children in care were clearly central to a child care officer's task but there was a wider spectrum of activity which included preventive work (Duties 1–3); recruiting carers (4+9); court duty (11–12); administration and finance (14+17); and aftercare (8+18).

Given the broad range of activity that Stroud outlines, the next question is: How did child care officers actually spend their time and with what balance of activity? Grey's (1969) study offers data on what child care officers were doing in nine local authorities in a particular fortnight in 1966.

Although the purpose of this research was 'to produce a formula for determining workloads and case composition', the study provides important evidence about the ratio of children under supervision to those in care. In 1966, there were 69,157 children in care in England and 43,845 supervised by child care officers. This ratio of 1.6 children in care for every one not in care and supported in the community contrasts vividly with today's figure. Currently in England, around six children receive support services while not in care for every one child who is looked after.

When the activity was disaggregated, Grey found that just over half (52%) of officers' time was spent on cases, 17 per cent on travelling and 31 per cent on general activities. Most time was devoted to children in care but 20 per cent was spent undertaking preventive work. In addition, some activities, such as the supervision of private foster homes, were a more important part of the workload than they are now. What is especially noticeable, however, is the time spent on cases by service directors, the children's officers – not surprising in terms of their remit under the 1948 legislation but unimaginable today.

It is difficult to make direct comparisons between these findings and the current situation in children's services because of changes in roles, legislation and organisation. However, some features of Stroud's (1965) list are recognisable, such as seeking resources for families, the amount of travel and paperwork and the difficulties of facilitating interagency collaboration.

Whether social workers spend as much time nowadays in direct contact with users is debatable but two major differences are likely to be the greater proportion of time spent in case conferences, mostly driven by child protection concerns but also by other children in need, and less joint work with voluntary agencies in areas like adoption and residential care.

What is striking in these comparisons is that the resources available to child care officers in the 1940s and 50s seem to have been remarkably slim – boarding out, residential care and their own commitment and energy. Increasing complexity of tasks and a growth in activity, accompanied by more potential resources, are the two most salient features of child care practice since 1948, although the barriers to effective practice seem no less formidable.

The changing practice context
From the mid-1970s, one can discern several strands in field social work activity that developed from the wider provision of services. For example, the publication of Rowe and Lambert's *Children who Wait* (1973), was followed by a move to specialise, as in fostering and adoption teams built on ideas of permanence, and a trend towards interprofessional collaboration. However, the most significant change in responsibilities affecting mainstream social workers occurred in child protection. A series of Inquiries followed child deaths throughout the 1970s and 1980s and extensive services were developed to protect children. But rather than resolve this by taking vulnerable children into care – although this is sometimes necessary – new approaches were developed to safeguard children who continued to live with their own families. This change of emphasis involved a process of 'refocusing', a policy designed to integrate social work approaches rather than view them as alternatives. Where separation was necessary, in contrast to much earlier practice, stays away from home became shorter and links with birth families and schools were maintained.

The Children Act 1989 and associated guidance provided the legal and conceptual framework to facilitate this shift and introduced extended arrangements for adoption and guardianship.

Social workers seemed to welcome such refocusing primarily because it provided a fresh opportunity to work with children, but it was inevitable that it would generate concerns. Indeed, Parton (1997) criticised the 'refocusing' approach for its lack of attention to how children's services had been caught up in the moral panic over child protection. He argued that the positivist scientific tradition had failed to grasp the wider political and economic pressures, which ensured that risk and risk insurance, rather than need, came to dominate the social work agenda. The fact that 'need' and 'child abuse' are social constructs was not in dispute; what the new thinking allegedly missed was the recognition that social work and wider public responses were similarly socially constructed.

At the same time, the value of evidence-based practice was being stressed by the Government. This demanded better information and stronger links between needs, thresholds, services and outcomes. Various materials, such as *Looking After Children* and the *Common Assessment Framework*, were developed to provide these and improve communication across agencies.

The situation in the last decade

The Labour Government post 1997 introduced a set of initiatives to address these issues by reorganising central administration, promoting interagency collaboration and encouraging best practice. While these changes were generally welcomed by social workers, they moved discussions about the nature of child and family social work in a new direction. The proposed changes focused on the prevention of social exclusion, community regeneration, improved parenting and the relief of poverty, and so promoted a range of services, many focused around schools and influenced by European pedagogic models.

To facilitate this shift in policy, the Government created local children's services departments, incorporating social services, education and parts of health, but not youth justice, which was kept separate. In a typical locality of 800,000 people, children's services departments employ some 15,000 people, most of whom are teachers (56%) or classroom assistants (33%), with only about 650 (4%) social workers.

While the aims of these policies echo those of social work in terms of improving society, there are contrasts in the roles envisaged with the 'traditional' casework approach. The responsibility for promoting welfare is now spread more widely across existing professions, such as teachers and doctors, and across new agencies, such as Youth Justice, SureStart, Connexions and groups of independent practitioners. This has led Parton (2009) to argue that social work roles have become more marginal, with narrower responsibilities for child protection and looked after children rather than wider family support, despite the fact that one of their skills is helping the 'hard-to-reach families' that are at the core of the Government's prevention policies.

Social work roles have also been affected by new technology as well as organisational change. Parton (2008) argues that this has changed the basis of professional knowledge from 'narrative' to 'database' information. While this makes decisions more transparent and accountable, knowledge is increasingly classified by database categories, such as risk and eligibility, at the expense of critical thinking and reflection.

While resistance to change is inevitable, some social workers say that external pressures are restraining them from providing what users need and want (Gupta and Blewitt, 2007). The imposition of bureaucracy and targets, the overriding concern with child protection and the frustration of being constrained from opportunities to undertake 'relational work' with children and families all produce dissatisfaction, and although training can help boost confidence and the ability to play a positive role, some social workers feel under-valued and beleaguered (Masson *et al*, 2008).

In an attempt to clarify how social work can best contribute to current policies, several observers, such as Blewett and colleagues (2007) and Hill (2010), have sought to identify the core components of social work. The first of these identifies seven (Blewett *et al*, 2007, p 6):

1. understanding the dynamic between the individual and the social;

2. combating social injustice;

3. transforming lives through relationship;

4. enabling people;

5. undertaking therapy;

6. managing risk to the community and the individual;

7. undertaking evidence-based practice.

In addition, they argue that the profession has to take a position on five axes: assessment and service delivery; proactive and reactive practice; centre-versus community-based work; promoting social and individual change; and care commissioning and provision (p 36). Hill echoes much of this but phrases the essential skills differently. He lists working in organisations, engaging with people, assessing and planning, court work, promoting change, ending, evaluating and reflective practice.

Discussion
It has been argued that an enduring concern in social work has been maintaining a balance of professional activities in a context where there is a tendency for assessment, planning, reviewing and negotiating to be undertaken at the expense of direct work with children. Certainly, most staff who provide services, such as residential or foster carers, continue to be less qualified than those professionals who request them.

The literature also indicates tasks for

which social workers are prime players and which they have been able to do relatively well. Alone, they may be insignificant in isolation but they could be highly relevant in the context of a wider intervention. One of these is improving people's relationships and behaviour, another is brokering on behalf of children, families and carers, both of which need to be complemented by an extensive range of supplementary skills.

Social work in the context of contemporary children's services
It seems likely that the future policy context of children's services in England will be one that encourages an increasingly professional approach to the fashioning of needs-led and evidence-based services, especially as these criteria appear to be an appropriate way of allocating scarce resources in a difficult economic climate. Equally important will be strategies that emphasise the benefits of seamless services, complementary approaches, varied provision arrangements and local initiatives. It is also clear that other services will be expected to deal with some of the problems normally considered to be the responsibility of social workers. So even if the role of social workers is clear, they will never have the monopoly of helping vulnerable children. In this situation, it is pertinent to ask what is special about child and family social work.

There is no doubt that the majority of child care activity – especially what is referred to as 'tending' – is undertaken by informal carers and ordinary families. Social workers have never been part of a universal service, despite the aspirations of the Seebohm Report (1968). Their role has been and will continue to be a specialised one, concentrating on those who are perceived to have fallen short of agreed parenting standards or are marked by unhappy family histories and ineffective social and kinship networks. The 'ordinary' resources that the majority take for granted are frequently lacking.

In such a situation, the personal disposition and qualities of practitioners are an important attribute and include such characteristics as specialist knowledge, experience, sensitivity and intelligence. But also important is being comfortable with the statutory role – that is, feeling sufficiently confident to ask questions that exceed the normal limits of social convention, to justify asking such questions and to have the skills to gain relevant and useful information. The difference from normal interaction is that this is not idle curiosity, which would be impertinence, but a purposeful inquiry conducted in a context where the skilled worker will assess what is left unsaid as well as the content and style of delivery of what is said. Once gathered, that information needs to be organised to inform a coherent service response.

While this might be insufficient to argue that social work expertise is 'unique', it is far from demonstrating that social work is just 'common sense'. Even if it were, the skill is to apply it appropriately – often to 'uncommon' situations. Thus, it is important to know what information is important, how to obtain it, how to interpret it and how to separate the vital from the tangential. Further skills are needed to select and fashion services; to link different aspects of people's lives, to connect the past, present and future, and understand which interventions are likely to help and why. Then there is the problem of implementing all of this. Because social workers are seeking to respond to children holistically but from within a confined agency perspective, their knowledge of what other agencies and professionals do and how to gain access to external resources is a core area of their expertise. Most parents act as their own 'brokers', identifying key resources and targeting their advocacy to ensure that what is needed for their child is actually delivered, but these abilities are not routinely available among many of the families with whom social workers deal.

Enduring difficulties of achieving and maintaining good practice have been revealed in this discussion of the chang-ing context of the social work role. These, it has been argued, have been exacerbated by the longstanding tendency for supervision and management tasks to take precedence over face-to-face work with service users, and the complexity of matching children's needs with interventions and outcomes. The problems of establishing unequivocal evidence on effectiveness mean that the value of the social work is always vulnerable to criticism from unsympathetic politicians and accountants. It is hoped that this historical perspective will help illuminate the struggles and achievements of organisations such as BAAF, which have sought answers to them.

References

Barclay P, *Social Workers: Their role and tasks*, London: Bedford Square Press, 1982

Bar-On A, 'Organisational resource mobilisation: a hidden face of social work practice', *British Journal of Social Work* 20:2, pp 133–149, 1990

Blewett J, Lewis J and Tunstill J, *The Roles and Tasks of Social Work: A literature informed discussion paper*, London: General Social Care Council, 2007

Challis L, *Organising Social Services*, Aldershot: Ashgate, 1990

Curtis (Chair), *Report of the Care of Children Committee*, Cmd 6922, London: HMSO, 1946

Grey E, *Workloads in Children's Departments*, London: The Home Office, 1969

Gupta A and Blewett J, 'Change for children? The challenges and opportunities for the children's social work workforce', *Child & Family Social Work* 12:2, pp 172–81, 2007

Hill A, *Working in Statutory Contexts*, Cambridge: Polity Press, 2010

Masson H, Frost N and Parton N, 'Reflections from the "frontline": social workers' experiences of post-qualifying child care training and their current work practices in the new children's services', *Journal of Children's Services* 3, pp 54–64, 2008

Parker R, *Away from Home: A history of child care*, Barkingside: Barnardo's, 1990

Parsloe P and Stevenson O, *Social Services Teams: The practitioner's view*, London: HMSO, 1978

Parton N, *Child Protection and Family Support: Tensions, contradictions and possibilities*, London: Routledge, 1997

Parton N, 'Changes in the form of knowledge in social work: from the social to the informational', *British Journal of Social Work* 38:8, pp 253–69, 2008

Parton N, 'From Seebohm to Think Family: reflections on 40 years of policy change of statutory children's social work in England', *Child & Family Social Work* 14:1, pp 68–79, 2009

Rowe J and Lambert L, *Children who Wait*, London: ABAA, 1973

Seebohm (Chair), *Report of the Committee on Local Authority and Allied Social Services*, Cmd 3703, London: HMSO, 1968

Stroud J, *An Introduction to the Child Care Service*, Harlow: Longmans Green, 1965

Fostering and Adoption in Scotland 1980–2010

Kirstie Maclean and **Barbara Hudson** identify differences in context, policy and practice, as well as the greater emphasis on children's rights and use of residential care, that distinguish Scotland from its neighbours 'down south'. Similarities and future aspirations for looked after children are also discussed.

Kirstie Maclean is Service Manager, Looked After and Accommodated Children, The City of Edinburgh Council

Barbara Hudson is Director of BAAF Scotland

Key words: adoption, fostering, Scotland, 1980–2010

Although the Act of Union came into force in 1707, Westminster continued to debate and pass separate Scottish domestic legislation until the devolved Scottish Parliament was established in 1999 and took over this role. This has inevitably led to a number of policy and practice differences, for instance Children's Hearings rather than courts for most child welfare and criminal cases, no custodial establishment for under-16s (although proportionally higher use of secure care), one of the lowest ages of criminal responsibility in the world (8) and gay and lesbian couples barred from fostering until 2009.

There is also a significantly different social, cultural and geographical context. Some examples are: much higher levels of parental drug and alcohol issues (2% to 3% of children in England and Wales and 4% to 6% of children in Scotland were estimated to have one or both parents affected by serious drug problems [Advisory Council on the Misuse of Drugs, 2003]); until recently, more outward than inward migration and relatively low numbers of black and minority ethnic inhabitants; and a land mass which, although half the size of England and Wales, has only one-tenth of the population. We have one local authority (Highland) which is the size of Wales and three tiny island authorities (Shetland, Orkney and Eilean Siar), all with populations of less than 27,000. Two further differences of emphasis have been a consistent, long-term focus on children's rights and greater use of residential care. Who Cares? Scotland was established in 1978 as an advocacy organisation run by and for looked after young people and has gone from strength to strength ever since. The Scottish Child Law Centre was established in 1989 and Scotland's Commissioner for Children and Young People was appointed in 2003. Residential care has had a more favourable reputation than in England and has not usually been seen as a 'last resort'. It has attracted both more government attention (eg Social Work Services Inspectorate [SWSI], 1992; Scottish Institute for Residential Child Care [SIRCC], 2010) and funding. (SIRCC, founded in 2000, is almost wholly government funded.)

In spite of these differences, many of the trends and developments in adoption and fostering over the last 30 years have mirrored those 'down south'. At times, Scotland has been in the forefront of change and development led by practitioners, academics or government, and at times it has lagged behind.

Permanence planning was being pursued in some areas of Scotland by 1980 (Lindsay Smith, 1979; McKay, 1980); different aspects were soon being examined, such as the timing of introductions (Kerrane, 1979), use of adoption allowances (Hill and Triseliotis, 1986; Triseliotis and Hill, 1987), placements of children with disabilities (Macaskill, 1988) and post-placement and post-adoption support services (O'Hara, 1986; Triseliotis, 1988; Hoggan, 1991; Lambert et al, 1992). Outcomes were increasingly considered (Fallon et al, 1983; Triseliotis, 1985; O'Hara and Hoggan, 1988; Hill et al, 1988; Borland et al, 1991).

Developments were also taking place in foster care in the 1980s and early 1990s, although, with the exception of Professor Triseliotis's prolific and invaluable research (eg Triseliotis, 1978, 1983 and 1989), this has been less well recorded. Specialist schemes for teenagers (O'Hara and Dewar, 1988) and for children with disabilities were established and new ways of working with children, such as group work, pioneered (Sim and O'Hara, 1982).

On the whole, the mid- to late 1990s and early years of the new century were considerably quieter periods for developments in foster care and adoption. There were probably a number of reasons for this: social work was to an extent on the back foot after some critical Inquiries (eg Orkney, Fife and Edinburgh); we were waiting for our new Acts (Children (Scotland) Act 1995 and Adoption and Children (Scotland) Act 2007), which frustratingly always seemed to take longer to achieve than legislation in England and Wales; and local government reorganisation in 1996 undoubtedly had a major impact. Moving from eight mainland and three island authorities to 32 local authorities meant not only that social workers were concentrating as much on their own futures as those of the children with whom they worked, but also that expertise was diluted and opportunities to specialise reduced.

Nevertheless, some pioneering work continued. Diana Part (1993) highlighted the crucial role of foster carers' own children and Marjut Kosonen (1994) emphasised the importance of sibling relationships. Research was undertaken on the impact of contact in adoption and on post-placement support (Stone, 1994; McGhee, 1998) and Donald Ramsay (1999) sought foster carers' views on recruitment and retention. Satnam Singh (1999) provided important insights into the assessment of Asian families in Scotland and John Triseliotis and colleagues (1999) researched why foster carers cease fostering.

The advent of the Scottish Parliament has allowed much greater focus on the needs and outcomes of looked after children than was previously the case. A characteristic of developments in foster care and adoption since 1999 is that they have been mainly government or government agency rather than practitioner or academic led. This shift of focus has generally been welcomed and there is now greater clarity of expectations, greater knowledge about outcomes and better quality assurance. A disappointment has been that there has been very little money put into social work research by the Scottish Government.

From the late 1990s, there was much greater concentration on the shortcomings of education of looked after children. This concentration started considerably later than in England and Wales, probably because 'there was a tendency to think we might be different – perhaps our looked after children were better served by an educational system widely considered to be in good shape' (Maclean and Connelly, 2005, p 173). Unfortunately, a review commissioned by the then Scottish Office (Borland et al, 1998) found that this complacency was unwarranted and that 'being looked after away from home in Scotland constituted an educational hazard' (Maclean and Connelly, 2005, p 173). This prompted an inspection of the education of children looked after away from home undertaken by Her Majesty's Inspectorate of Education and the Social Work Services Inspectorate. Some evidence was found that children's experiences and outcomes, although not good enough, were not as poor as expected (Maclean and Gunion, 2003). The two inspectorates and the Scottish Government commissioned a number of studies and development materials (eg Connelly, 2003; Connelly et al, 2003; Hudson et al, 2003) This has been followed up by two Scottish Government guides (Scottish Executive, 2007; Scottish Government, 2008) setting out how we 'can and must do better' in the education of looked after children and also the roles and responsibilities of corporate parents. Educational outcomes are improving but only very slowly (Connelly and Chakrabarti, 2007). There is very limited information on the educational outcomes of adopted children (Phillips, 2007).

Two further areas of focus in the last two decades have been the health of looked after children and young people (eg Minnis and Del Priore, 2001; The

Residential Care Health Project, 2004) and improvement of after care services (Dixon and Stein, 2002; Scotland's Commissioner for Children and Young People [SCCYP], 2008). Since 2004, looked after children's nurses and specialist CAMHS services for looked after children, where they have been established, have definitely improved health care. There is less evidence of improvement in aftercare services.

The Scottish Commission for the Regulation of Care (the Care Commission) was established in 2002 and annual fostering and adoption inspections were piloted in 2005. They have been fully in place since 2006/07. This was the first time that local authority fostering and adoption services had been inspected. A year on, the Care Commission reported a range of strengths in services but also a number of weaknesses, especially around timescales for carer/adopter recruitment, reviews of foster carers, written documentation and quality assurance (Scottish Commission for the Regulation of Care, 2007). The Scottish Government established the Adoption Policy Review Group which reported in 2002 and 2003 (Scottish Government, 2002, 2003). This led not only to the Adoption and Children (Scotland) Act 2007 but, combined with recommendations made in *Getting it Right for Every Child in Kinship and Foster Care* (Scottish Government, 2009), led to major changes in the Looked After Children (Scotland) Regulations 2009. In particular, these strengthened the role and support of kinship carers. While this Act and Regulations have brought welcome developments, the opportunity has been missed to commission research into their implementation and impact.

What of Scotland's aspirations for the future? We must ensure that the principles of permanence planning are sustained in both policy and practice. Any child who cannot be safely brought up within his or her family should have the opportunity to experience nurture, care and hope for the future with individuals and families who will be there 'as a family of resource' past the end of

childhood. To achieve this, we believe that further attention must be given to the legal framework for making these life-changing decisions. The current legal journey, for many looked after children, is a tortuous progress through Children's Hearings to the Sheriff's Court. Even if local authorities are proactive in their planning processes, the operation of Children's Hearings is not one that facilitates permanence planning. The Sheriff's Court does have this focus, but does not have child and family work as a dedicated area of practice. Fundamental change may be necessary as a response to increasing numbers of children requiring the state to protect and promote their welfare.

A similar radical approach is needed towards those individuals and families who foster or adopt. Making and sustaining relationships, providing nurture and unconditional love are fundamental to caring for damaged and vulnerable children. However, training and a range of supports can enhance these qualities and must continue to be offered as an integral part of family placement services. Greater professional recognition of carers would have the potential to provide both external respect and validation of the skills they offer. Just as important for the future will be ensuring that the philosophy and practical applications of adoption support, laid out in the Adoption and Children (Scotland) Act 2007, are embedded in practice.

As described in this article, making and achieving effective long-term plans for children can be a fragile activity, vulnerable to changes in fashion, personnel, structure and resources. If improved services are to be delivered for children, we need to ensure that the conditions which appear to have pertained in the 1980s, namely energetic and pioneering practice, strong partnerships between practitioners and researchers and support for innovation from government and employers, are restored. In Scotland it is possible, quite literally, for those leading adoption and fostering practice to come together for a common purpose. Hopefully, our shared vision and commitment will ensure that in another 30 years family placement practice will be 'getting it right for every child'.

References

Advisory Council on the Misuse of Drugs, *Hidden Harm: Responding to the needs of children of problem drug users*, Report of an Inquiry by the Advisory Council on the Misuse of Drugs, 2003

Borland M, O'Hara G and Triseliotis J, 'Placement outcomes for children with special needs', *Adoption & Fostering* 15:2, pp 18–28, 1991

Borland M, Pearson C, Hill M, Bloomfield I, *Education and Care Away from Home: A review of policy, practice and research*, London: Scottish Council for Research in Education, 1998

Connelly G, 'Developing Quality Indicators for Learning with Care', *Scottish Journal of Residential Child Care* 2:2, pp 69–78, 2003

Connelly G, Mackay E and O'Hagan P, *Learning with Care: Information for carers, social workers and teachers concerning the education of looked after children and young people*, University of Strathclyde, 2003

Connelly G and Chakrabarti M, 'Can Scotland achieve more for looked after children?', *Adoption & Fostering* 31:1, pp 81–91, 2007

Dixon J and Stein M, *Still a Bairn: Throughcare and after care services in Scotland*, Edinburgh: Scottish Executive, 2002

Fallon M, McKenna M, Waring P, Wilson G, Thom M and Giltinan D, 'Placing adolescents in families', *Adoption & Fostering* 7:4, pp 43–46, 1983

Hill M and Triseliotis J, 'Adoption allowances in Scotland', *Adoption & Fostering* 10:4, pp 11–19, 1986

Hill M, Hutton S and Easton S, 'Adoptive parenting – plus and minus', *Adoption & Fostering* 12:2, pp 17–23, 1988

Hoggan P, 'Attitudes to post-placement support services in permanent family placement', *Adoption & Fostering* 15:1, pp 28–30, 1991

Hudson B, Furnivall J, Paterson S, Livingston K and Maclean K, *Learning with Care: Training materials for carers, social workers and teachers concerning the education of looked after children and young people*, University of Strathclyde, 2003

Kerrane A, 'Timing the introduction', *Adoption & Fostering* 96:2, pp 23–25, 1979

Kosonen M, 'Sibling relationships for children in the care system', *Adoption & Fostering* 18:3, pp 30–35, 1994

Lambert L, Borland M, Hill M and Triseliotis J, 'Using contact registers in adoption searches', *Adoption & Fostering* 16:1, pp 42–45, 1992

Lindsay Smith C, 'Monitoring New Families Project', *Adoption & Fostering* 95:1, pp 14–17, 1979

Macaskill C, 'It's been a bonus – families' experience of adopting children with disabilities', *Adoption & Fostering* 12:2, pp 24–30, 1988

Maclean K and Connelly G, 'Still room for improvement? The educational experiences of looked after children in Scotland', in Crimmens D and Milligan I (eds), *Facing Forward: Residential child care in the 21st Century*, Lyme Regis: Russell House Publishing, 2005

Maclean K and Gunion M, 'Learning with care: the education of children looked after away from home by local authorities in Scotland', *Adoption & Fostering* 27:2, pp 20–31, 2003

McGhee J, 'Consumers' views of a post-placement support project', in Hill M and Shaw M (eds), *Signposts in Adoption: Policy, practice and research issues*, London: BAAF, 1998

McKay M, 'Planning for permanent placement', *Adoption & Fostering* 99:1, pp 19–21, 1980

Minnis H and Del Priore C, 'Mental health services for looked after children: implications from two studies', *Adoption & Fostering* 25:4, pp 27–38, 2001

O'Hara G, 'Developing post-placement services in Lothian', *Adoption & Fostering* 10:4, pp 38–42, 1986

O'Hara G and Dewar C, 'Fostering teenagers – what works for whom and why', *Adoption & Fostering* 12:2, pp 38–42, 1988

O'Hara G and Hoggan P, 'Permanent substitute family care in Lothian – placement outcome', *Adoption & Fostering* 12:3, pp 35–39, 1988

Part D, 'Fostering as seen by carers' children', *Adoption & Fostering* 17:1, pp 26–30, 1993

Phillips R, 'The need for information on how the attachment difficulties of adopted and looked after children affect their schooling', *Adoption & Fostering* 31:3, pp 28–38, 2007

Ramsay D, 'Recruiting and retaining foster carers', in Hill M (ed), *Signposts in Fostering:*

Policy, practice and research issues, London: BAAF, 1999

Scotland's Commissioner for Children and Young People (SCCYP), *Sweet 16? The age of leaving care in Scotland*, Edinburgh: SCCYP, 2008

Scottish Commission for the Regulation of Care, *The Quality of Fostering and Adoption Services in Scotland*, Edinburgh: Care Commission, 2007

Scottish Executive, *Looked After Children and Young People: We can and must do better*, Edinburgh: Scottish Executive, 2007

Scottish Government, *Adoption Policy Review Group Report, Phase 1*, Edinburgh: Scottish Government, 2002

Scottish Government, *Adoption Policy Review Group Report, Phase 2*, Edinburgh: Scottish Government, 2003

Scottish Government, *These are our Bairns: A guide for community planning partnerships on being a good corporate parent*, Edinburgh: Scottish Government, 2008

Scottish Government, *Getting it Right for Every Child in Kinship and Foster Care*, Edinburgh: Scottish Government, 2009

Scottish Institute for Residential Childcare, *National Residential Child Care Initiative*, Edinburgh: SIRCC, 2010

Sim M and O'Hara G, 'Group work with children who are joining new families', *Adoption & Fostering* 6:4, pp 31–37, 1982

Singh S, 'Assessing Asian families in Scotland', in Hill M (ed), *Signposts in Fostering: Policy, practice and research issues*, London: BAAF, 1999

Social Work Services Inspectorate, *Another Kind of Home: A review of residential child care*, London: HMSO, 1992

Stone S, 'Contact between adopters and birth parents: the Strathclyde experience', *Adoption & Fostering* 18:2, pp 36–38, 1994

The Residential Care Health Project, *Forgotten Children: Addressing the health needs of looked after children and young people*, NHS Lothian, 2004

Triseliotis J, 'Growing up fostered', *Adoption & Fostering* 94:4, pp 11–23, 1978

Triseliotis J, 'Identity and security in adoption and long-term fostering', *Adoption & Fostering* 7:1, pp 22–31, 1983

Triseliotis J, 'Adoption with contact', *Adoption & Fostering* 9:4, pp 19–24, 1985

Triseliotis J and Hill M, 'Children and adoption allowances', *Adoption & Fostering* 11:1, pp 35–39, 1987

Triseliotis J, 'Adoption services and counselling', *Adoption & Fostering* 12:2, pp 31–37, 1988

Triseliotis J, 'Foster care outcomes: a review of research findings', *Adoption & Fostering* 13:3, pp 5–17, 1989

Triseliotis J, Borland M and Hill M, 'Foster carers who cease to foster', in Hill M (ed), *Signposts in Fostering: Policy, practice and research issues*, London: BAAF, 1999

BAAF's role in the development of the foster care service

June Thoburn and **Gillian Schofield** demonstrate how the development of the foster care service over the last 30 years reveals BAAF's varied points of engagement with policy and practice, which have increasingly helped to shape the foster care agenda.

June Thoburn is Emeritus Professor of Social Work, University of East Anglia

Gillian Schofield is Professor of Child and Family Social Work, University of East Anglia

Key words: foster care, policy and practice, history, BAAF

Foster care 30 years ago

A foster parent's role must always depend on which aspects of the parental role are still being exercised by the natural parents and which are being undertaken by the agency. The foster parents' difficult task is to fill in the gaps so that the child's needs are met without unnecessary overlapping of function.
(Rowe, 1977, p 15)

Jane Rowe wrote the article 'Fostering in the seventies' shortly before she 'signed off' as Director of the Association of British Adoption and Fostering Agencies (ABAFA) and moved to an equally crucial role in assisting government by both undertaking and synthesising child welfare research. In the article she characterises foster care at the end of the 1970s as essentially a 'parent supplement' service. For each child, the role of the foster carers was to meet those needs (especially their needs for good-quality parenting) that the birth parents were not able to meet, and for as long as required. She recognised that, for some carers, this meant taking on a full 'care and upbringing role' until the child reached adulthood and, in some cases, on into adult life ('foster parents' rather than 'foster carers' was the most frequently used term). However, in very few cases would this mean that birth parents had no role to play as their children grew up.

Rowe established that the majority of children living with foster families at any point in time would be in 'longer-term' or 'care and upbringing' place-ments, but that the majority of children who at any time in their lives experi-enced foster care would be with foster *carers* fulfilling a short-term role for a specific, short-term purpose. The concept of foster care careers rather than foster care as an undifferentiated service was already firmly established by the start of the 1980s when ABAFA became BAAF and *Adoption & Fostering* was relaunched as the major UK vehicle for the publication of practice and research articles.

Throughout the next 30 years, BAAF (through workshops, training events and especially its book publishing arm and *Adoption & Fostering*) has encouraged research and reported on developments in foster care. This 'intelligence' has been used both to encourage develop-ments in practice and to work with local authorities, the 'third sector' and govern-ment to achieve positive change in the service for children, birth families and carers. An aspect of this work that we shall comment on is the changing emphasis BAAF has placed on its dual role of championing both adoption and foster care. Although for BAAF (in its 'lobbying' role) there have been changes of emphasis, this has been less marked with respect to the organisation's pub-lishing arm, which throughout the period has been a vehicle for publications on all aspects of child placement policy and practice. We would like to pay tribute, here, to the role of Sarah Curtis, editor of *Adoption & Fostering* from 1976 to 1987, in keeping her ear to the ground and commissioning contributions from the broad spectrum of child welfare research, as well as sifting through submitted articles, a tradition built on by the editors that followed her.

The 1980s

During the period leading up to the Children Act 1989, BAAF's London fostering project (BAAF, 1982) resulted in definitions of six types of short-term and two types of long-term foster family placement (four if custodianship and long-term kinship care are included).

There was a large element of consensus about the short-term aims of 'rehabilitation', 'preparation for permanence' through adoption, 'bridge to independence' for older children or treatment foster care. Nancy Hazel had already brought back from Sweden and introduced initially to Kent Social Services Department a 'professional fostering' scheme, providing defined-length placements mainly for teenagers (described in her seminal 1981 text, *A Bridge to Independence*).

In contrast, the respective roles of adoption and 'care and upbringing' foster care placements for children who could not return to their families was more contested territory. In the wake of the Rowe and Lambert (*Children who Wait*, 1973) report of ABAFA-initiated research on children who remained for long periods in unplanned and often unstable care, and of reports from the US of successful adoption placements of older and otherwise 'hard-to-place' children, long-term foster care had already, in 1980, been overshadowed by the drive to 'special needs' adoption. In the light of recent developments, it is also interesting to note that numbers placed in foster care with relatives were also in decline. By and large, BAAF during this period, especially in its lobbying activities, became identified with championing adoption and the importance of time limits during which this should be achieved (see especially the influential article by Hussell and Monaghan, 1982). The championing of foster care was largely left to the National Foster Care Association (NFCA), a body which at that time not only emphasised the professionalisation of foster care but also, in that context, task-centred rather than 'family for life' fostering.

As a result, long-term foster care was, politically speaking, 'in the doldrums' for much of this decade. It was left to the Family Rights Group (FRG) and to the Dartington research team led by Spencer Millham and Roger Bullock (1986) to articulate the importance of links with birth families for children in long- as well as short-term care. The (in retrospect unhelpful) polarisation around the weight to be placed on links with birth parents was played out in BAAF's *Terminating Parental Contact* (Adcock and White, 1980) and the FRG's response, *Fostering Parental Contact* (Family Rights Group, 1982).

This situation arose despite the fact that foster care research and practice had made some important steps forward, with *Adoption & Fostering* very often 'scooping' the early articles and dissemination events. Some of the voluntary sector specialist permanent placement agencies (notably Barnardo's' Barkingside project led by Joan Fratter) placed children for both permanent foster care and for adoption, with differing degrees of birth family contact in sufficient numbers for these to be evaluated by Thoburn and Rowe (1988). They concluded from this longitudinal study of over 1,100 children, mostly placed when aged three or older, that when the characteristics and any difficulties of the children were held constant, there was no statistically significant difference in the likelihood of placement disruption between those placed with the intention of permanent foster care and those placed with the intention of adoption. They also concluded that continuing parental contact was either a neutral or a protective factor and Thoburn's (1985, p 30) *Adoption & Fostering* article identified eight 'routes to permanence'.

As can be seen from the above, the publications wing of BAAF (sometimes in an important partnership with Batsford Publishers) continued to publish research on long-term foster care, including that by Jane Rowe and colleagues (1984). This identified both strengths and weaknesses in practice and pointed to some necessary changes, some of which found their way into the Children Act 1989 and even foreshadowed important changes made by the Children and Young Persons Act 2008. The video *It's Like a Bereavement* (Hundleby, 1984) was a powerful product of this research, documenting the poor quality of much of the work with birth parents of children in foster care during this period. Informed by the early work on this project, Jane Rowe was commissioned by BAAF to synthesise research, policy and practice in *Fostering in the Eighties* (1983). In both of these publications she pointed to the important role of kinship foster carers, reporting, for the first time, generally more positive outcomes than for non-kinship carers. Also, along with the Select Committee (House of Commons Social Services Committee, 1984), Bill Jordan (1981) and Olive Stevenson (1980), she articulated a note of caution about the tendency to see permanence as synonymous with adoption, to the exclusion of improved practice in foster care and reunification:

The emphasis on permanence sharpens perceptions about what can and should be done to offer security within the framework of fostering as well as through adoption. (Rowe, 1983, p 20)

There would appear to be some danger that this established resource (long-term fostering) will be completely repudiated before adequate efforts have been made to identify the group of children for whom it still may be the placement of choice and without proper consideration of ways in which fostering could be improved. (Rowe, 1983, p 30)

By the end of the 1980s, most local authorities had taken their lead from the pioneering voluntary agencies and had set up their own adoption agencies, separate from their fostering teams, and long-term fostering tended to fall between the two. Much of BAAF's effort on training and guidance materials went into providing training and conferences for these adoption teams. The BAAF forms E and F, developed largely as tools for the assessment of adopters and the

permanence needs of children, began to be 'stretched' for the assessment of foster carers. At the end of the decade, the large-scale Rowe *et al* (1989) study of almost 10,000 placements built on the BAAF fostering project and quantified the proportions of children placed in different sorts of foster care and the differential 'success rates' for these different aims. Thirteen per cent of nearly 4,000 recent placements were for 'care and upbringing' and over two-thirds of these were rated as 'successful'. The majority were placed with one of six short-term/task-focused aims.

The 1989 legislation sought to achieve a balance between family support and children's need for protection and a sense of permanence if long-term care became necessary. Also during the decade, the reduction in residential group care placements had led to children in foster care having more complex problems, accentuated by the increase in issues of addiction and domestic conflict among the parents of children needing placement. Another key development during this period, largely springing from adoption-focused work but importantly influencing child welfare as a whole and foster care in particular, was BAAF's role in powerfully articulating the needs of children with disabilities and children of minority ethnic heritage (continued throughout these 30 years).

The 1990s

The Children Act 1989 emphasised placement in care or accommodation as part of a family support service (see Department of Health, 1989; Packman and Hall, 1998; Aldgate and Bradley, 1999 on the benefits to parents and children of well-managed short-term care services). However, for the first half of the 1990s, foster care as a whole received little government attention, although NFCA published training materials, recommendations on allowances and in 1999, the (Department of Health recommended) *National Foster Care Standards*. This was especially the case for long-term fostering, which was still not considered in most local authorities and in government guidance as a 'permanence option'. If anything, attitudes to long-term fostering were in a worse state towards the end of the 1990s than in the 1980s, with the dominant discourse being about children 'lingering' and 'languishing' in foster care.

Around the middle of the decade, research reports and the increasing strength of the voices of young care leavers and foster carers themselves gradually gave voice to the neglect suffered while in care of those for whom neither return home nor adoption were appropriate. In particular, they highlighted the multiple placement changes and the fact that too many young people were leaving care around the age of 16, having become detached from birth families but not made links with new families. Towards the end of the decade the *Quality Protects* initiative (Department of Health, 1998) finally sought to introduce some urgency and resources into all aspects of placement policy and practice.

The general pattern of BAAF's lobbying and development work in the 1980s continued through most of the next decade, if anything with the emphasis on adoption enhanced by a growing pessimism about the potential of the care system to be of benefit, and especially by the strong support for increasing adoption from care provided by Tony Blair when New Labour came into government in 1997 (see Performance and Innovation Unit, 2000). However, BAAF publications and *Adoption & Fostering* continued to report on the many research and often small-scale practice developments, especially in foster care, with renewed interest in a range of 'professional' foster care projects, this time imported from the USA rather than Europe (Chamberlain and Reid, 1998; Walker *et al*, 2002). BAAF's publications, training and development activities played important roles in the development of respite fostering for children with disabilities, and it was among the few bodies that focused on the needs of privately fostered children and their carers.

However, the independent sector built on the early 'professional fostering' work of Nancy Hazel and stepped in to meet the growing demand for foster placements that local authorities were unable to meet from their own resources (charted by Sellick, 1999 and more recently – forthcoming). BAAF responded to this development by hosting a special interest group.

The 2000s

By 2000, the renewed focus on all types of placement brought in by *Quality Protects* was beginning to take effect, with the *Choice Protects* initiative (Department of Health, 2002) to promote fostering also contributing to the debates and actions leading to *Care Matters* (Department for Education and Skills, 2006) and the Children and Young Persons Act 2008. Towards the end of the decade, a more balanced view about the positives as well as the negatives of out-of-home placement began to be reported (see Bullock *et al*, 2006). Much of the research was conducted by members of BAAF's Research Group Advisory Committee or showcased at BAAF-hosted dissemination events. Of particular importance among these were studies by Lowe, Murch *et al* (2002) and by Selwyn *et al* (2006), as they demonstrated that many of the children for whom a 'family for life' placement was needed found this, if they were going to do so, through a permanent foster family placement. The BAAF-published research by Schofield and Beek (Schofield *et al*, 2000; Schofield, 2003) also showed that when a 'sense of permanence' was a guiding principle, permanent foster care could take its place alongside adoption as a placement of choice. At the same time, research by Sinclair and colleagues (2007) and Farmer *et al* (2004) with respect to teenagers demonstrated that instability in foster care continued and was sometimes created by the reluctance to recognise that children who had put down roots should not be moved for pragmatic reasons, and that an inflexible approach to leaving care planning might be preventing some young people from remaining part of their foster families well into adult life.

BAAF's policy focus on foster care in the context of permanence broadened with its landmark piece of work undertaken in partnership with the Fostering Network on the financing of foster care (Tapsfield and Collier, 2005).

From 1998, with the arrival of Felicity Collier, John Simmonds and later David Holmes, the further strengthening of BAAF's research support and publications activities led to a broadening of the focus of its lobbying work. The emphasis on placement stability for all who needed long- or short-term care, or were 'on the edges of care' was central to the approach taken to lobbying and development work. BAAF gave cogent evidence to the Select Committee Inquiry on looked after children (House of Commons, 2009) and *Care Matters* (Department for Education and Skills, 2006). In broadening its focus, BAAF became recognised as a major 'home' for all those seeking to improve services for children needing care or on the edges of care.

The appointment of a specific fostering development consultant contributed to a range of fostering initiatives. Work with the Maudsley team led not only to the *Fostering Changes* programme (Pallet *et al*, 2005) but also to an innovative practice development project focused on children's learning and literacy (Pallett *et al*, 2010). A further partnership with the Centre for Research on the Child and Family at the University of East Anglia led to a Big Lottery-funded BAAF project on planning for permanence in foster care that also resulted in new practice guidance (Schofield and Beek, 2008).

Conclusion

The recent range of BAAF fostering projects has led to research books and articles, practice guides, training manuals, national conferences and the active use of research-based materials by BAAF consultants and trainers with practitioners in all four UK countries. It

has required partnerships across the policy, practice and academic research communities in order to make best use of BAAF's role as a catalyst for action on the fostering agenda. This diversity of activity and knowledge transfer in foster care, alongside consistently high levels of consultation and lobbying, demonstrate how active BAAF has become in influencing policy, research and practice in foster care.

References

Adcock M and White RAH (eds), *Terminating Parental Contact: An exploration of the issues relating to children in care*, London: ABAFA, 1980

Aldgate J and Bradley M, *Supporting Families through Short-term Fostering*, London: The Stationery Office, 1999

BAAF, *A Comprehensive Adoption Service for London: The voluntary contribution – a discussion paper*, London: BAAF, 1982

Bullock R, Courtney M, Parker R, Sinclair I and Thoburn J, 'Can the corporate state parent?', *Children and Youth Services Review* 28:11, pp 1344–58 (reprinted in *Adoption & Fostering* 30:4, pp 6–19, 2006

Chamberlain P and Reid J, 'Comparison of two community alternatives to incarceration for chronic juvenile offenders', *Journal of Consulting and Clinical Psychology* 66:4, pp 624–33, 1998

Department for Education and Skills, *Care Matters: Transforming the lives of children and young people in care*, London: TSO, 2006

Department of Health, *The Children Act 1989: Principles and Practice in Regulations and Guidance*, London: Department of Health, 1989

Department of Health, *Quality Protects*, London: TSO, 1998

Department of Health, *Choice Protects*, London: TSO, 2002

Family Rights Group (eds), *Fostering Parental Contact*, London: Family Rights Group, 1982

Farmer E, Moyer S and Lipscombe J, *Fostering Adolescents*, London: Jessica Kingsley Publishers, 2004

Hazel N, *A Bridge to Independence*, Oxford: Blackwell, 1981

House of Commons Children, Schools and

Families Committee, *Looked After Children*, London: TSO, 2009

House of Commons Social Services Committee, *Report: Children in Care*, HC 380, 1984

Hundleby M, *It's Like a Bereavement*, Video, Barkingside/London: Barnardo's/BAAF, 1984

Hussell C and Monaghan B, 'Child Care Planning in Lambeth', *Adoption & Fostering* 6:2, pp 21–25, 1982

Jordan B, 'Achieving permanence: Papers from Swanick 1981: Prevention', *Adoption & Fostering* 5, pp 20–22, 1981

Lowe M and Murch M, Borkowski M, Weaver A, Beckford V with Thomas C, *The Plan for the Child: Adoption or long-term fostering*, London: BAAF, 2002

Millham S, Bullock R, Hosie K and Haak M, *Lost in Care*, Aldershot: Gower, 1986

National Foster Care Association, *The National Foster Care Standards*, London: NFCA, 1999

Packman J and Hall C, *From Care to Accommodation: Support, protection and care in child care services*, London: The Stationery Office, 1998

Pallett C, Blackeby K, Yule W, Weissman R and Scott S, *Fostering Changes: How to improve relationships and manage difficult behaviour: A training programme for foster carers*, London: BAAF, 2005

Pallett C, Simmonds J and Warman A, *Foster Carer Education Programme: Supporting Learning – helping foster carers to improve children's reading*, London: BAAF, 2010

Performance and Innovation Unit, *Prime Minister's Review of Adoption*, London: The Cabinet Office, 2000

Rowe J, 'Fostering in the seventies', *Adoption & Fostering* 90:4, pp 15–20, 1977

Rowe J, *Fostering in the Eighties*, London: BAAF, 1983

Rowe J and Lambert L, *Children who Wait*, London: ABAA, 1973

Rowe J, Cain H, Hundleby M and Keane A, *Long-term Foster Care*, London: Batsford/BAAF, 1984

Rowe J, Hundleby M and Garnett L, *Child Care Now – A survey of placement patterns*, London: BAAF, 1989

Schofield G, *Part of the Family: Pathways through foster care*, London: BAAF, 2003

Schofield G and Beek M, *Attachment for Foster Care and Adoption*, London: BAAF, 2006

Schofield G and Beek M, *Achieving Permanence in Foster Care: A good practice guide*, London: BAAF, 2008

Schofield G, Beek M, Sargent K and Thoburn J, *Growing up in Foster Care*, London: BAAF, 2000

Sellick C, 'Independent fostering agencies: providing high quality services to children and carers?', *Adoption & Fostering* 24:1, pp 7–14, 1999

Sellick C, 'Independent fostering providers: predators or pioneers, partners or procured?', *Adoption & Fostering*, forthcoming

Selwyn J, Sturgess W, Quinton D and Baxter C, *Costs and Outcomes of Non-infant Adoptions*, London: BAAF, 2006

Sinclair I, Baker C, Lee J and Gibbs I, *The Pursuit of Permanence: A study of the English care system*, London: Jessica Kingsley Publishers, 2007

Stevenson O, 'Family problems and patterns in the 1980s', *Adoption & Fostering* 4:2, pp 20–24, 1980

Tapsfield R and Collier F, *The Cost of Foster Care: Investing in our children's future*, London: BAAF/Fostering Network, 2005

Thoburn J, 'What kind of permanence?', *Adoption & Fostering* 9:4, pp 29–34, 1985

Thoburn J and Rowe J, 'A snapshot of permanent family placement', *Adoption & Fostering* 12:3, pp 29–39, 1988

Walker M, Hill M and Triseliotis J, *Testing the Limits of Foster Care: Fostering as an alternative to secure accommodation*, London: BAAF, 2002

The challenges in planning for permanency

Julie Selwyn highlights the importance of recognising children's positive relationships and ensuring that children are connected to adults who will offer a long-term commitment.

Julie Selwyn is Reader and Director of the Hadley Centre for Adoption and Foster Care Studies at the School for Policy Studies, University of Bristol

Key words: planning for permanency, adoption, children's relationships

The principles of 'planning for permanency' have been around a long time. In England, the initial impetus to permanency planning came from the finding that there were large numbers of children drifting in the care system without plans made for their futures (Rowe and Lambert, 1973). At about the same time, psychologists were highlighting the poor developmental outcomes for children in care who drifted without attention paid to their relationships. The classic text *Beyond the Best Interests of the Child* (Goldstein *et al*, 1973) laid out three principles of planning:

• Placement decisions should safeguard the child's need for continuity of relationships . . .

• Placement decisions should reflect the child's not the adult's sense of time . . .

• Child placement decisions must take into account the law's incapacity to supervise interpersonal relationships and the limits of knowledge to make long-range predictions.

Looking again at these principles more than 30 years later, they are still as relevant today as they were in the 1970s. Indeed, a great deal of subsequent research has reinforced the importance of understanding how children's early relationships affect well-being throughout the lifespan.

Yet, the vision of a planning process that actively supported children's relationships was never realised. Very quickly, permanency planning became synonymous with making a plan for adoption and the focus on safeguarding children's *relationships* was replaced by an emphasis on finding a *placement*. Perhaps this was because the death of Maria Colwell in 1973 and the subsequent Inquiry heralded an era where the emphasis was on assessing risk, and the structures and organisations social workers operated in became increasingly legalistic and procedural. During the 1980s, permanency planning became discredited in the UK, partly because of the almost exclusive association with adoption but also because services to support birth families were severely lacking. Research, however, continued to highlight the lack of attention given to children's relationships in care planning. For example, a Dartington study (Millham *et al*, 1986) showed how children in care often had no meaningful links with their birth families and that the connections had withered away, leaving them isolated and without adequate support networks.

The late 1990s saw a renewed interest in permanency planning. Once again, children drifting in care, poor developmental outcomes and a build-up of long-term looked after children put pressure on the care system and sparked concerns. Another Inquiry, this time into the abuse of children in care (Waterhouse, 2000), led to a governmental review of adoption policy and practice (Performance and Innovation Unit, 2000), which was quickly followed by new legislation: the Adoption and Children Act 2002. Guidance (Department for Children, Schools and Families, 2002) stressed the importance of permanency planning in reducing delay in decision-making and in securing better outcomes for children through the timely planning of a permanent placement secured by a legal order. In practice, permanency planning again quickly became associated with a one-off event – a placement and primarily an adoptive placement. The principle of ensuring *all* children had positive adult relationships that were able to offer life-long support was lost again and the popularity of adoption moved backwards and forwards on the seesaw of placement options.

Perhaps this came about because the importance of understanding and working with relationships (what used to be termed casework) became unfashionable. Instead, social workers became case managers, referring on work that once they would have done themselves; supervision became focused on whether tasks had been completed within a set timescale rather than on understanding the processes, systems and dynamics of working with families. The families themselves became reduced to 'service users' (or, even worse, described as 'users'). Indeed, the importance of the continuity in the relationship between the worker and the child or family was given little weight in planning, as administrative arrangements dominated decisions about when children's cases were transferred between teams. Yet, having secure positive relationships over time is at the heart of normal healthy development.

The continuity of relationships and life-long connections

Research has shown that having a network of positive social relationships means that as adults we are likely to have higher self-esteem, do better at school, be employed and have a greater sense of well-being and better health (Fursentenberg and Hughes, 1995; Scholte et al, 2001). Children need connections to adults committed to their welfare. For children abused and neglected these connections provide a buffer from the risks and vulnerabilities they carry and enable them to use the 'social scaffolding' that enduring adult relationships provide (Massingham and Pecora, 2004).

Therefore, the challenge of permanency planning is not simply to find a placement but to ensure that *every* child and young person has lifelong connections to people who will continue to offer positive relationships and support. The social work role in enabling and supporting these relationships is crucial,

as is the belief that it is *never too late* to find such relationships. Of course, children's relationships can be secured by providing support and returning children to their birth families or by placing with kin. However, many children cannot be reunified and alternative positive adult relationships need to be secured.

Adoption

Finding an adoptive family is one way to provide new positive adult relationships. Research (Rushton, 2003) has shown the remarkable improvements in children's development as a result of having loving family care. Over the last 30 years, there have been many challenges to practices that exclude certain groups of children or prospective adopters from being considered for adoption, but there is evidence that some unhelpful practice continues.

It is difficult to know exactly how many children are not found an adoptive family, although it could be as many as a quarter of those with adoption recommendations. The primary reason is a lack of suitable adopters but also perhaps 'good-enough' families are being turned away. There is still suspicion of foster carers who wish to adopt and of 'non-traditional' adopters such as single parents, gay/lesbian carers (Hicks, 2005) and adopters whose motivation is not driven by infertility. In some areas of the country, prospective minority ethnic adopters are not being assessed if their ethnicity and religion does not 'match' that of waiting children. In all other regards, they might make excellent parents for the many waiting white and minority ethnic children with adoption recommendations. Reluctance to pay an interagency fee or provide adequate financial support to adopters also restricts choice. There is evidence that some social workers are pessimistic about children's futures and have beliefs about which children are adoptable and that this results in reduced family-finding activity (Cousins, 2009; Selwyn et al, 2010).

The child's age is one reason why

adoption may not be considered. Finding adoptive homes for older children is more challenging but usually not impossible and late-placed children can have very good outcomes (Rushton et al, 2000; Selwyn et al, 2006). The numbers of those adopted older than four years has been decreasing (Department for Education, 2009) – perhaps because younger children are easier to place and therefore local authority adoption targets are easier to meet. However, also acting as a disincentive is a belief that because the risk of disruption increases with the child's age at placement, adoption should not be attempted. It should be noted that the finding that 'the older the child the greater the risk of disruption' also holds true for children reunified with birth parents (Farmer, 2009), and those placed with kin (Hunt, 2009) and with foster carers (Sinclair, 2005). Indeed, adoption placements are usually more stable than foster and kinship care (Sinclair, 2005; Hunt, 2009; Biehal et al, 2010).

During the last 30 years, there have also been rapid developments in understanding the links between brain development and behaviour (Glaser, 2000; Tomalski and Johnson, 2010). Perry and colleagues' work (1995) on the impact of severe neglect on infant brains has become particularly well known and has led to some practitioners feeling fatalistic about the life chances of children who enter care after many years of abuse and neglect. However, we are many years away from being able to predict with any certainty those problems that progress from childhood to adulthood (Masten et al, 2004).

Less well known is the research showing that there is a significant period of brain growth during late adolescence and early adulthood (Masten et al, 2004; Avery and Freundlich, 2009). There is growing evidence that this later development period provides an important window of opportunity whereby what appeared to be a deviant pathway can be changed.

Long-term foster care

Even if every effort is made, many children will not be found adoptive families and others will not want to be adopted. Long-term foster care should be able to provide the connections and lifelong relationships that these children need, but some children remain in unhappy but 'stable' placements, while others move around the care system and are never found positive secure relationships with adults (Sinclair, 2005). Research has shown that children who grow up in a stable foster family (kin or stranger) are generally doing as well as adopted children educationally and have similar levels of mental health difficulties when measured during early adolescence (Schofield, 2009; Biehal et al, 2010). However, current policy and practice are undermining the progress children have made.

Unlike young people in adoptive families, many of those in long-term foster care are expected to manage the enormous challenges that are involved in becoming an adult without much support. Studies have shown that visits from social workers decline and only about a third of foster carers continue to provide some help as young people leave care (Stein and Munroe, 2008; Wade, 1997, 2008). It is therefore not surprising that research has highlighted the poor outcomes for young people who lack the safety net of a family and the social support for a successful transition to adulthood. The evidence suggests that it is essential that young people are able to stay connected to adults, with whom they have positive relationships, during early adulthood.

Searching for lost connections and making new relationships

There is evidence from innovative projects in the US (Landsman et al, 1999; Louisell, 2009; Avery, 2010) that it is possible to find families for young people at risk of leaving care unconnected to adults. In these projects, new families were often identified through mapping and searching young people's past and current networks. Many of these searches were *led by the young person* and it was they who identified people already in their life who might become a potential permanent family. Sometimes this was birth family members or relatives with whom they had lost contact, or previous carers or professionals such as residential workers or teachers, who were willing to offer the necessary long-term commitment to the young person. Relationships were secured sometimes by adoption but not always. Importantly, the workers in these projects had a strong value base, tenacity and a belief that finding adults willing to offer the necessary commitment was possible.

Three immediate points spring from the US experience. First, the engagement of the young person in the search was crucial to the success of this approach. It has been previously noted (Sinclair, 2005) that children can make or break placements depending on whether they want to be there, but in the UK we have been slow to allow young people to lead. Second, it was necessary to identify young people's networks and important relationships. Most of these young people were placed successfully with people they already knew. There seems to be resistance or suspicion in the UK if a teacher, social worker, foster carer or health professional who knows the young person steps forward and asks to be considered. It is almost as though they have crossed a boundary and become 'unprofessional'. Third, it highlights the importance of the social worker's value base and their persistence in achieving the objectives. It is clear that the possibilities for children and young people should not be limited simply because they are older, of minority ethnicity, or disabled.

How might practice change in the UK?

Making permanency planning a reality would involve prioritising the maintenance and support of children's networks and relationships at every review. It is surprising that one study recently found that social workers were not always aware of who were the important people in a young person's life (Wade, 2008). Without this basic knowledge, it is difficult to envisage how permanency planning could begin. It has been argued that permanence is a 'state of mind not a placement' (Stuart Foundation, 2002). But, we need to ask, 'Whose state of mind?' If planning for permanence continues to be 'achieved' in social workers' minds by finding a placement, it is likely that targets will continue to dominate and children will continue to leave care unconnected to supportive adults.

We need a shift in focus to prioritising children's relationships and putting the need for a stable secure relationship back at the top of the hierarchy of need. The expertise and skills currently used for child appreciation days could be adapted to consider the networks of long-term looked after children. Birth families should not be discounted, as with the passage of time they might be able to offer a home (Masson *et al*, 1999). Family group conferencing could also be used at different points in a young person's life, as a way of identifying important adults.

So, the challenges ahead are to make permanency planning a reality by first ensuring that children's positive relationships are recognised and supported. These relationships may be with siblings, family members, present and previous foster carers, or other professionals. Second, we should not allow any child or young person to leave care without connections in place to adults who are willing to offer lifelong support. It should never be too late for a child or young person's relationships to be supported and secured. Third, we need to see a reassertion of the importance of relationships in social workers' own day-to-day work and the understanding that it is through relationships that it is possible to bring about positive change in people's lives.

References

Avery RJ, 'An examination of theory and promising practice for achieving permanency for teens before they age out of foster care', *Child-*

ren & Youth Services Review 32, pp 399–408, 2010

Avery RJ and Freundlich M, 'You're all grown up now: termination of foster care support at age 18', Journal of Adolescence 32, pp 247–57, 2009

Biehal N, Ellison S, Wade J, Sinclair I, Dixon J and Richards A, Characteristics, Outcomes and Meanings of Three Types of Permanent Placements: Adoption by strangers, adoption by carers and long-term foster care; available at www.adoptionresearchinitiative.org.uk/study1.html, 2010

Cousins J, 'Disability: Still taboo in family placement?' Adoption & Fostering 33:2, pp 54–65, 2009

Department for Children, Schools and Families, Adoption Guidance: Adoption and Children Act 2002; available at www.everychildmatters.gov.uk

Department for Education, 'Children looked after in England including adoption and care leavers year ending March 31st 2009'; available at www.dfe.gov.uk

Farmer E, 'Reunification with birth families', in Schofield G and Simmonds J (eds), The Child Placement Handbook, London: BAAF, 2009

Furstenberg F and Hughes E, 'Social capital and successful development among at-risk youth', Journal of Marriage and the Family 57, pp 580–92, 1995

Glaser D, Child abuse and neglect and the brain: a review, Journal of Child Psychology and Psychiatry 41:1, pp 97–116, 2000

Goldstein J, Freud A and Solnit J, Beyond the Best Interests of the Child, New York: Free Press, 1973

Hicks S, 'Lesbian and gay foster care and adoption: a brief UK history', Adoption & Fostering, 29:3, pp 42–56, 2005

Hunt J, 'Family and friends care', in Schofield G and Simmonds J (eds), The Child Placement Handbook, London: BAAF, 2009

Landsman MJ, Malone K, Tyler M, Black J and Groza V, Achieving Permanency for Teens: Lessons learned from a demonstration project, Prevention Report, 2, 1999 [Online]. http://www.uiowa.edu/~nrcfcp/services/publication/fall1999.htm

Louisell MJ, 'Six steps to find a family: a practice guide to family search and engagement (FSE)', 2009; available at http://centerforchildwelfare.fmhi.usf.edu/kb/Prgprac/Six%20Steps%20to%20Find%20a%20Family.pdf

Massingham R and Pecora J, 'Providing better opportunities for older children in the child welfare system', The Future of Children 14:1, pp 151–73, 2004

Masson J, Harrison C and Pavlovic A (eds), Lost and found: making and remaking working partnerships with parents of children in the care system, London: BAAF, 1999

Masten A, Burt K, Roisman Obradovic J, Lond J and Tellegen A, 'Resources and resilience in the transition to adulthood: continuity and change', Development and Psychopathology 16, pp 1071–94, 2004

Millham S, Bullock R, Hosie K and Haak M, Lost in Care, London: Gower, 1986

Performance and Innovation Unit, Prime Minister's Review of Adoption, London: The Cabinet Office, 2000

Perry B, Pollard R, Blakley T, Baker W and Vigilante D, 'Childhood trauma, the neurobiology of adaptation, and "use-dependent" development of the brain: how states become traits', Infant Mental Health Journal 16, pp 271–91, 1995

Rowe J and Lambert L, Children who Wait, London: ABAA, 1973

Rushton A, Knowledge Review: The adoption of looked after children, London: Social Care Institute for Excellence, 2003

Rushton A, Dance C and Quinton D, 'Findings from a UK-based study of late permanent placements', Adoption Quarterly 3:3, pp 51–71, 2000

Scholte J, van Lieshout M and van Aken G, 'Perceived relational support in adolescence: dimensions, configurations and adolescent adjustment', Journal of Research on Adolescence 11, pp 71–94, 2001

Schofield G, 'Permanence in foster care', in Schofield G and Simmonds J (eds), The Child Placement Handbook, London: BAAF, 2009

Selwyn J, Sturgess W, Quinton D and Baxter C, Costs and Outcomes of Non-infant Adoptions, London: BAAF, 2006

Selwyn J, Quinton D, Harris P, Wijedasa D, Nawaz S and Wood M, Pathways to Permanence for Black, Asian and Mixed Ethnicity Children: Dilemmas, decision-making and outcomes, London: BAAF, 2010

Sinclair I, Fostering Now, London: Jessica Kingsley Publishers, 2005

Stein M and Munro E (eds), Young People's Transitions from Care to Adulthood: International research and practice, London: Jessica Kingsley Publishers, 2008

Stuart Foundation, 'Stuart Foundation convening 17–19 April, 2002: Permanence for older children and adolescents'; available online at http://www.stuartfoundation.org/convening.html

Steinberg L, 'Cognitive and affective development in adolescence', *Trends in Cognitive Science*, 9:2, pp 69–74, 2005

Tomalski P and Johnson MH, 'The effects of early adversity on the adult and developing brain', *Current Opinion in Psychiatry* 23, pp 233–38, 2010

Wade J, 'The ties that bind: support from birth families and substitute families for young people leaving care', *British Journal of Social Work* 38:1, pp 39–54, 2008

Wade J, 'Developing leaving care services: tapping the potential of foster carers', *Adoption & Fostering* 21:3, pp 40–9, 1997

Waterhouse R, *Lost in Care*, London: Department of Health, 2000

Thinking on developmental psychology in fostering and adoption

Alan Rushton discusses thinking over the last 30 years in developmental psychology as it affects fostering and adoption. He charts significant progress in six areas and assesses BAAF's contribution to various aspects of this accumulating knowledge.

Alan Rushton is Visiting Professor, Institute of Psychiatry, King's College, London

Key words: adoption, fostering, developmental psychology

Introduction

The last 30 years have seen remarkable progress in the science of developmental psychology. Much of it has contributed to, but has also been challenged by, the field of adoption and fostering. The study of children at high risk of psychosocial problems moving into unrelated families has clearly provided the context to pursue such investigations.

A considerable gulf once existed between the worlds of developmental psychology and child welfare studies: the former interested in normal and abnormal development and more recently, in the question of persistence of problems or the capacity for recovery from adversity. Researchers with a background in child welfare studies have, on the other hand, mostly pursued questions about the consequences of different placement policies. They have asked how various arrangements – for example, foster care *versus* adoption, late *versus* early placement, siblings placed together or apart, with and without birth family contact – have influenced optimum development. These worlds have gradually been moving closer together, in part because developmentalists have realised that there is much to learn from studies of children whose parenting has been severely disrupted, and in part because child welfare researchers need more detailed and informative indicators of the psychosocial outcomes for such children.

We have thus been able to profit over the decades from the accumulating evidence on outcomes of alternative family care. Some (very) broad-brush findings have now been established; for example, that orphanage care is generally harmful for development (Gunnar and van Dulmen, 2007) and that domestic infant adoptions are likely to be highly stable and successful and the adults well adjusted (eg Collishaw *et al*, 1998). On the other hand, special needs children, late placed from care, although successful in most cases, may have persistent difficulties in continuing adoptive placements (Rushton and Dance, 2006). Follow-ups of the psychological well-being of former foster children into adulthood are still not as common as adoption studies but tend to show worse outcomes than for comparable young adults. For example, one-third of the young people placed in foster family care following abuse and neglect who were interviewed in a recent large-scale US study were suffering from a variety of mental health problems, alcohol or substance misuse (Courtney and Dworsky, 2006).

Although these generalised findings need qualification, in essence, the more the rearing environment offers warm, sensitive, individualised, predictable care, generating a feeling of personal security about the present and future, the better the outcome. The implications have therefore become much clearer for securing positive environments for children.

In considering the contribution of developmental psychology, it stands as only one perspective among many related to family placement and, within that, only selected aspects can be presented here. I have selected six areas, largely those related to behavioural, emotional and social development. Topics like memory, cognition, educational achievement and executive function will receive little attention.

1. Developmental consequences of early adversity

A crucial area of developmental research in adoption and fostering is the exploration of adverse early environments and their consequences, notably in relation to institutional rearing and maltreatment. How much do the effects of early adversity persist even when the child is subsequently raised in more favourable circumstances? A major burst of new data has appeared with the systematic follow-up of ex-orphanage children (from the sending countries of Asia, Latin America, Africa and Eastern Europe) into adoptive homes in the world's richer nations. In some ways, the initial pessimism about outcomes has given way to qualified optimism due to the extraordinary (but not complete) developmental catch-up (eg Rutter and the ERA study team, 1998).

These follow-up studies have encouraged fresh thinking on the multiple range of influences on development. The factors that precede the adoptive or foster care placement, including genetic and perinatal factors, child temperament and the earlier parenting experiences, have a part to play in later outcomes. A difficulty here is that such information is rarely captured, or even accessible, in samples of young children relinquished or separated from birth parents and subsequently placed in new families.

Such research has also forced a greater specification of the nature of the early adversity. In order to understand what kinds of negative experiences are related to ill-effects, we need to know: what degree of deprivation was experienced; what kind of needs were neglected – eg nutritional or interactional; and what was the type of abuse, the severity and duration. The more that is known of the specific characteristics of the adverse environment, the more these can be linked to specific difficulties and the phases of the lifespan at which they appear.

The past 30 years have seen the growth of understanding of the full range of psychosocial problems of maltreated children. The prevalence of disorder for children in care in the UK has been shown to be strikingly high – five times greater than in non-disadvantaged private households (Ford et al, 2007). Furthermore, it has become clear that although problems of maltreated children can occur in any domain (behavioural, social, emotional, cognitive), conduct problems tend to predominate (impulsivity, over-activity, oppositional behaviour, attentional problems, temper tantrums, and sometimes serious aggression) as well as disturbed attachment patterns or slowness to attach to new carers, indiscriminate sociability and lack of trust. The immense challenges presented to their new carers have slowly become more recognised.

2. The long view of development

The study of developmental psychology, once concerned mainly with birth to adolescence, now covers the complete lifespan. New data sources have made possible longer-term prospective longitudinal studies – a much more productive design than purely descriptive or retrospective studies. However, only very few studies have so far been able to take this long view of adoption (eg Tieman et al, 2005).

Longer-term follow-up studies are revealing more about adjustment and mental well-being. Researchers have begun to ask how persistent are any ill-effects, or is there an attenuation of the connection between early experience and full adulthood? What quality of adult intimate relationships follow from early distorted attachment? What is the effect on parenting? How does early adversity influence the capacity to adapt to change, to regulate emotion, to respond appropriately to stress? Cognitive components of adult development are highly important as are existential issues for the adopted person.

Despite the narrowing of the gulf, developmental and family placement research can sometimes seem as far apart as ever. It can be baffling to encounter a follow-up study from childhood abuse and neglect to later in life but with an absence of information on the consequence of these adversities being detected. Was the abuse intra- or extra-familial? Was it followed by removal from or return home, by unstable public care, or successful permanent family placement? Such factors are likely to be crucial to understanding any association with adult outcome.

A shift has taken place away from a sole focus on predictors of negative outcome and towards the examination of those interesting groups with high early adversity but with normal or better than normal adult outcome. Concepts of resilience and protective factors have assumed great importance. Some children adapt better than others to negative treatment, to moves and to settling in to a permanent new home. Research-based knowledge on what developmental pathways are possible has encouraged taking the longer-term view of the need for appropriate support services.

3. Attachment
The influence of attachment theory has been immense in child placement – first, in understanding the consequences of broken and distorted attachments and later, in how far secure attachment can be achieved in the new adoptive or long-term foster home. Early predictions ranged from doubts about the capacity of children to re-attach to unrelated carers or conversely, to undue optimism about the restorative value of a family placement. Recent studies using the technique of meta-analysis have provided more solid evidence on age of placement in relation to the risk of insecure attachment (van den Dries et al, 2009). However, the burst of attention devoted to attachment has by no means come to rest and debate is still sharp among developmentalists about the conceptualisation and classification of attachment patterns and methods of reliable assessment (O'Connor and Zeanah, 2003).

Attachment theory, having become the dominant language of placement planning and decision-making, is too large a field to tackle here. However, one cautionary point may be worth making:

some factors may pre-date or exert an influence independently of the child's relationships and we should perhaps be more cautious about assuming that what is presented is indeed the expression of a problematic attachment history. Social relationship problems and aggression may be related, for instance, to parental alcohol misuse or to taking both psychiatric and illicit drugs during pregnancy, in which case any planned intervention may need to be conceived differently.

4. Developmental psycho-therapists
One strand of thinking that has been of considerable, if not primary, importance for practitioners seeking insight into children's developmental needs, is the work of the 'developmental psycho-therapists', as some choose to call themselves: from the USA, Vera Fahlberg, Dan Hughes and Nancy Verrier; and from the UK, Caroline Archer, Sheila Fearnley and Kate Cairns – to name only some of the most prominent. Their contribution to understanding developmental processes comes from an individual, therapeutic perspective, often theorising from their experiences of problematic placements referred to specialist centres and clinics. They have focused on how early losses, traumatic separations and unplanned transitions may have held back placement progress; how unresolved grief and loss may inhibit the growth of fresh attachment. Their contributions have been influential but caution is commonly advised in generalising about developmental processes from such clinical samples. Talk of the 'universal consequences' of maltreatment is not advisable, as children in families not seeking services may have followed more positive developmental pathways due to resilience, or to protective factors or unexpectedly rapid developmental recovery. As an example, Collishaw et al (2007) showed that a substantial minority of abused children did not have any mental health difficulties in adult life.

5. Genetics, brain development and the neurobiological basis of behaviour

The overlapping and fast-emerging field of neuropsychology deserves a mention. Advances in the field of human genetics, neurobiology and brain development have begun to provide better understanding of the biological basis of persistent psychosocial problems. In the context of maltreatment, genetic differences may influence either susceptibility to, or reduced risk of, later mental health problems. The new tools, such as brain neuro-imaging, may elucidate the link between maltreatment, brain development and behaviour, the body's stress response system, and possible psychiatric problems (see McCrory *et al*, 2010 for a recent update). However, it will perhaps be some time before we know whether these are enduring changes to the brain and how, more precisely, they relate to abnormal behaviour, and much further along the line, whether this understanding will lead to any generally agreed placement implications.

A useful explanatory concept, bridging psychology and neurodevelopment, is the notion of adaptation: that the developing child facing stress or deprivation makes adaptive responses, biological and psychological, which at the time may have a useful survival function but may not serve the individual well in a more benign (family placement) environment.

6. Measuring developmental problems and progress

I remember as a psychology undergraduate being required to write an essay entitled 'The discipline of psychology advances by means of its tools'. Support for the truth of this proposition comes in the benefit of an expanding variety of assessment tools in this field. In the first wave of placement follow-up research, outcomes were often limited to new carer satisfaction ratings or were defined in terms of simple continuity of placement (regardless of quality). Now, validated measures of children's difficulties are required in research and used,

to a variable extent, in practice (eg the Strength and Difficulties Questionnaire, Goodman, 2001; the Assessment Checklist for Children, Tarren-Sweeney, 2007). Well-known assessments such as the Strange Situation Procedure are being followed by new assessments of attachment and indiscriminate friendly behaviour. Behaviour patterns are beginning to be related to DNA analysis and to measures of diurnal cortisol production (the stress hormone). Along with multiple measures taken at many points in time, more advanced statistical methods for modelling developmental changes have had to be devised (Ferrer and McArdle, 2010).

Although great progress has been made in improving on previous gross measures of functioning, measurement has further to go in capturing the complex problem profiles of maltreated children and children in transition to a new home, especially in capturing positive attributes and detecting perhaps small but highly meaningful change. A gradual shift has been evident from a deficit model of problem checklists to identifying strengths and adaptability, endearing as well as challenging characteristics.

However, the perspective of *individual* child psychology has limitations in application to adoption and fostering. An interactional concept like 'goodness of fit' has come to be more useful in placement planning, involving not just the child's strengths and difficulties and the new carers' characteristics, but the likelihood of a 'good match' between them. The favourable combination will be where a family placement can provide stable, supportive care and where the child has the capacity to profit from this new environment. One study of this kind has explored children's adaptation to a new placement in relation to their 'internal representations' of significant people and the adoptive mother's attachment style (Henderson *et al*, 2003).

Adoption and foster care studies may have played a part in the search for a greater understanding of social influences on personal development. We have witnessed the growing importance of identity studies (adoption identity, personal and ethnic identity) and the study of discrimination and racism on attitudes to the self. The early studies of transracial placements were heavily criticised for relying on standard mental health measures alone and taking less account of the concepts of personal and ethnic identity. Such criticism has prompted attempts to capture the complex notion of ethnic identifications and their relationship with psychological adjustment and self-worth.

BAAF's contributions in relation to developmental psychology

Having presented these six selected aspects of developmental psychology, I now turn to ways in which BAAF has acted as a conduit for carrying these advances to the world of adoption and fostering practice. BAAF has always had children's optimum development at the heart of its enterprise and supported the dissemination of relevant developmental theory and research. It has been the publishing outlet of choice for many UK researchers wishing to convey the findings of their original studies to a broad audience. Some of the early publications began to report on original research and not all were uncontentious (eg Gill and Jackson [1983] on transracial placements). Many of these publications were concerned with developmental progress and outcomes.

Numerous authors, in the pages of *Adoption & Fostering*, have risen to the challenge over the years of elaborating developmental models, applying concepts of attachment and resilience theory to family placement and publishing studies assessing psychological adjustment of life in foster or adoptive families. Both smaller-scale intensive studies as well as surveys based on large databases have appeared.

BAAF staff have also had an important input into government ventures like the Adoption Research Initiative and its Research Advisory Group has played a significant role here. Composed of active researchers, it has provided a forum for examination of new research, discussion of methodological issues and consideration of the validity of research claimed to support new policies and practices. This group could perhaps have become more proactive and taken on tasks like scoping recent developments in adoption and fostering research and putting forward priorities for a research agenda, especially those with a human development focus.

BAAF's annual research conferences have played a key role in disseminating good-quality research and helping practitioners to become more research minded. In addition, the organisation has hosted the Health Group meetings, workshops and group seminars across the four BAAF regions. Topics have frequently covered early deprivation, drawing on contributions from psychology and child psychiatry. More recently, BAAF has hosted a number of original research projects like the studies by Ivaldi (2000) on adoptions patterns, on search and reunion (Triseliotis *et al*, 2005) and the follow-up of Hong Kong Chinese infants adopted into the UK in the 1960s (Feast *et al*, 2009).

Conclusions

The research effort in corralling data to track the developmental status of children with unfavourable early environments in subsequent family placements has surely brought benefits. But by no means all these advances have found their way into practice. Nor, with much more complex modelling of developmental causes and consequences, are we much closer to predicting outcome in individual cases. Slowly increasing knowledge of developmental patterns should at least assist in presenting more realistic expectations to carers, in estimating a likely timescale for difficulties to attenuate and in tailoring more effective placement preparation and support.

References

Collishaw S, Maughan B and Pickles A, 'Infant adoption: psychosocial outcomes in adulthood', *Social Psychiatry and Psychiatric Epidemiology* 33:2, pp 57–65, 1998

Collishaw S, Pickles A, Messer J, Rutter M, Shearer C and Maughan B, 'Resilience to adult psychopathology following childhood maltreatment: evidence from a community sample', *Child Abuse & Neglect* 31, pp 211–29, 2007

Courtney M and Dworsky A, 'Early outcomes for young adults transitioning from out-of-home care in the USA', *Child & Family Social Work* 11:3, pp 209–19, 2006

Feast J, Rushton A, Grant G and Simmonds J, 'Work in progress: the British Chinese Adoption Study (BCAS)', *Adoption & Fostering* 33:4, pp 68–70, 2009

Ferrer E and McArdle J, 'Longitudinal modeling of developmental changes in psychological research', *Current Directions in Psychological Science* 19:3, pp 149–54, 2010

Ford T, Vostanis P, Meltzer H and Goodman R, 'Psychiatric disorder among British children looked after by local authorities: comparison with children living in private households', *British Journal of Psychiatry* 198, pp 319–25, 2007

Gill O and Jackson B, *Adoption and Race*, London: Batsford/BAAF, 1983

Goodman R, 'Psychometric properties of the Strengths and Difficulties Questionnaire (SDQ)', *Journal of the American Academy of Child and Adolescent Psychiatry* 40, pp 1337–45, 2001

Gunnar M and van Dulmen M, 'Behavior problems in post-institutionalized internationally adopted children', *Dev Psychopathol* 19:1, pp 129–48, 2007

Henderson K, Hillman S, Hodges J, Kaniuk J and Steele M, 'Attachment representations and adoption: associations between maternal states of mind and emotion narratives in previously maltreated children', *Journal of Child Psychotherapy* 29:2, pp 187–205, 2003

Ivaldi G, *Surveying Adoption: A comprehensive analysis of local authority adoptions 1998–1999*, London: BAAF, 2000

McCrory E, De Brito S and Viding E, 'Research review: the neurobiology and genetics of maltreatment and adversity', *Journal of Child Psychology and Psychiatry* 51:10, pp 1079–95, 2010

O'Connor TG and Zeanah C, 'Current perspectives on assessment and treatment of attachment disorders: Special issue', *Attachment and Human Development* 5:3, pp 221–325, 2003

Rushton A and Dance C, 'The adoption of children from public care: a prospective study of outcome in adolescence', *Journal of the American Academy of Child and Adolescent Psychiatry* 45:7, pp 877–83, 2006

Rutter M and the English and Romanian Adoptees (ERA) study team, 'Developmental catch-up, and deficit, following adoption after severe global early deprivation', *Journal of Child Psychology and Psychiatry* 39:4, pp 465–76, 1998

Tarren-Sweeney M, 'The Assessment Checklist for Children (ACC): a behavioral rating scale for children in foster, kinship and residential care', *Children and Youth Services Review* 29, pp 672–91, 2007

Tieman W, van der Ende J and Verhulst F, 'Psychiatric disorder in young inter-country adoptees: an epidemiological study', *American Journal of Psychiatry* 162, pp 592–98, 2005

Triseliotis J, Feast J and Kyle F, *The Adoption Triangle Revisited: A study of adoption, search and reunion experiences*, London: BAAF, 2005

van den Dries L, Juffer F, van IJzendoorn M and Bakermans-Kranenburg M, 'Fostering security? A meta-analysis of attachment in adopted children', *Children and Youth Services Review* 31, pp 410–21, 2009

Assessment Changes in thinking and practice

Margaret Adcock discusses the considerable changes that have taken place in the nature, content and process of assessments since the 1960s and, in particular, over the past three decades.

Margaret Adcock was Assistant Director, Education and Training at BAAF, 1975–84, then a social work consultant

Keywords: assessment, fostering, adoption, permanence, planning

Assessment has always been an integral part of both fostering and adoption. But, the nature, content and process of assessments have changed very considerably over the years in the light of the different kinds of children needing placement and different methods of finding families for them.

BAAF and its predecessors have contributed enormously to these changes, always being 'ahead of the game' and inviting pioneers in new thinking and practice to speak and train at conferences. This has been complemented by publications and articles in *Adoption & Fostering* and contributions from the legal and medical (now health) groups.

Among the individuals who have been particularly influential in their contribution to thinking and practice in the field of assessment and preparation are David Kirk, Kay Donley, Phyllida Sawbridge, Vera Fahlberg, Nessie Bailey, Margaret McKay, Linda Katz and, most recently, Jennifer Cousins. All of them have considered the interaction between parents/substitute parents and children rather than focusing just on the assessment of adults or the child. Their ideas and practice have established the framework necessary to ensure making good placements.

What has the term 'assessment' meant in practice? Four different definitions are relevant:

• appraisal;

• the act of assessing, especially in Britain, the evaluation of a student's achievement on a course;

• a process of gathering and documenting information;

• evaluation: a judgement about something based on an understanding and analysis of the situation.

Assessment practice in adoption, and to a large extent fostering, has moved over the years from simple appraisal of applicants in the late 1960s, to preparation – a course of education, information and support for applicants and the child – to assessment and, finally, to evaluation.

This development is apposite, as Howe (1998) has explained that the outcomes of adoption are largely the result of a series of complex psychological interactions between three major relationship experiences:

• the quality of pre-placement biological parent–child relationships;

• the quality of post-placement adoptive parent–child relationships;

• the interpretation of what it means to be adopted by the adopted child (and possibly by his or her parents).

The 'how' and 'when' to do assessments have also had a significant effect, for better and for worse, on these relationships and their interactions (see Barth and Berry, 1988; Selwyn *et al*, 2006)

Changes in the assessment process of applicants

In the late 1960s, when adoption in the UK was mainly of healthy white illegitimate babies by childless couples, the main focus of assessment was on the prospective carers. There was a screening or appraisal process often known as 'vetting'. The criteria were not revealed to applicants although an adoption worker in the late 1960s described to me the ideal applicants as 'emotionally stable, financially secure, married couples with no skeletons in the cupboard'!

Adoptive parents were not, however, happy with the role ascribed to them. In *Shared Fate* (1964) David Kirk, a sociologist and adoptive parent, described the challenges and dilemmas adoptive families faced. He said that public sentiment perceived the nature of adoptive parenthood as second best, but if the adoptive family denied the fact of adoption and pretended to be just like other families, it created difficulties for itself. Adopters who could admit that they had missed an important experience because of their infertility were more likely to be able to think about the original birth parent. Adoptive parents needed education and support for their special task.

Mia Kellmer Pringle, Director of the National Children's Bureau, developed this theme in a lecture in 1971 and suggested that:

. . . evaluation should be supplemented, if not supplanted, by preparation, including information about child development, the kinds of children needing adoption and meeting with established adopters. The primary aim would be to achieve self-selection. (Kellmer Pringle, 1976, pp 60–61)

In the 1970s, agencies began to look for adopters who would offer homes to older and disabled children, usually from care. It was thought that the provision of a loving home would help deprived and damaged children to heal. Prospective carers were now seen as a valuable resource and had to be treated as such. This highlighted both the preparation element of assessment and the necessity of new ways of providing this.

The Adoption Resource Exchange (ARE), set up in 1970, became closely involved in the structure and administration of adoption services and produced a standardised form E to provide information about a child needing a family and a Form F to be the basis of referral for an interagency exchange but also for the presentation of a completed home study to the agency panel (Ruber, 1977).

Kay Donley (1975) told UK adoption agencies that what applicants for older and special needs children needed and wanted was preparation and help in the task they were offering to take on. Most people were capable of deciding for themselves whether or not they could take on a given task, provided they were fully informed as to what might be involved and were offered adequate support in doing it.

Inherent in this concept of preparation was the idea that applicants could change and grow during the process of assessment and placement, and that agencies have a responsibility to help them do this.

This was very much the philosophy of Parents for Children, a new agency set up in 1976 to seek parents for older and disabled children whom no other agency had yet been able to place. The director said the objective was to offer preparation rather than investigation. The approach was to find parents for each child individually rather than building up a bank of adopters. Applicants would initially be given information, followed by open meetings, group discussions, contact with experienced carers and interviews to clarify the aims and methods of the agency and give descriptions of the children on referral. Education was provided about the specific child. Many people would weed themselves out if they found this was not for them and those who continued at least understood fairly clearly the kind of parenting that was being sought and could themselves be involved in the decision as to whether they were capable of doing it (Sawbridge, 1980).

Barnardo's New Families project, set up in Glasgow in 1976, had a similar approach. They said:

We set off with no rigid criteria – many of those accepted are independent, highly mobile people with strong religious or moral convictions and not much concerned about what the neighbours think. This is in strong contrast to our expectations of well adjusted, problem free, semi rural couples well supported

by generations of family and friends.
(Lindsay Smith, 1980, p 200)

In an article entitled 'Task-centred assessment for foster parents', Davis *et al* (1984) stated that applicants had come to offer a service and were not expecting to engage in a therapeutic encounter. The application process in their agency involved both a five-session group, which provided information about reasons for care, child development, problems of foster children, birth families and consideration of the skills needed for fostering, and a home study. The group used participants' own experience and knowledge, which provided a supportive atmosphere for sharing and learning. Newly approved foster parents had expressed a sense of having some shared responsibility for the final panel decision.

Over the years, the content of the information that has to be absorbed by adoptive and fostering applicants has greatly expanded. So, too, has the detail of the individual assessments now required in the Prospective Adopter and Foster Parent Reports (Chapman, 2009; Dibben, 2010). This is partly due to child protection concerns, but also arises from research about the development of adoptive families which pointed to the need, where possible, to select adoptive parents with secure attachment status and without unresolved loss issues (Steele *et al*, 2003). Standardised assessment measures such as the Adult Attachment Interview (AAI) and the Attachment Style Interview (ASI) are now increasingly being advocated. There seems to be a greater focus on individual assessments of adults and children, rather than on the interaction between the agency, the carers, the child and the birth parents, which had previously been at the heart of assessment practice.

Cousins (2010), trying to find more families for the many children still waiting in care, has now returned to a focus on interaction. She has re-introduced the idea of giving adopters an increased opportunity in the preparation process to see and hear about 'real' children rather

than just being told what their characteristics might be.

The assessment of children

For an interagency placement, the Adoption Resource Exchange required a profile of the child together with a description of the preparation and direct work with him/her. In the words of Donley (1975, p 23):

The older the child at the time of presentation for placement, the more damaged s/he may be. Therefore it is absolutely imperative that the worker placing the child has seen him in action.

Donley said information also had to be gained from people who knew the child well. Records needed to be examined and a detailed history of traumatic experiences, changes and moves compiled. Direct work had to be done to prepare the child:

Only the child who knows his past and has integrated it into his whole life experience will be free enough to move into successful placement with a substitute family. By the end, the placement worker should be able to make some reasonable predictions of the child's future. (Donley, 1975, pp 30–31)

Subsequently, BAAF staff developed a training pack titled *In Touch with Children* (Bailey and Batty, 1984) and devoted a lot of time and energy to helping placement workers improve their skills in direct work with children.

Over 14 years from 1980, Vera Fahlberg taught a new generation of UK social workers the importance of understanding and assessing attachment issues in adoption, and how to identify developmental issues and work with disturbed children and their carers. She said the worker's role was to identify how and where the child was 'stuck' developmentally and then work with families to create strategies for continued growth and change, thus helping the child to become 'unstuck' (Fahlberg, 1984).

This excellent level of assessment and

preparation of children has apparently not been sustained on a widespread basis. Dance et al (2010) reported that one in six agencies did not get basic factual information correct in children's assessment forms. In over half of all agencies, the quality of reports was described as poor or not of consistently good quality.

Assessment of birth parents

Despite the efforts to place children from care for adoption, work with birth parents to prevent children coming into or remaining in care unnecessarily in the 1970s was characterised by delay, indecision and lack of leadership from senior management. Then in 1979, a Scottish social worker, Margaret McKay, told a packed audience at a BAAF conference that no child under ten in her authority had remained in care for more than two years. A new method of assessing and working with birth parents had been developed and children were returning home or being adopted. The crucial time to work with such parents was the first six months after the child came into care.

The essence of this method (McKay, 1980) was a philosophy that:

• No child should grow up without people he or she looked on as parents – birth parents or permanent parent substitutes – who could provide good enough care to meet his or her needs.

• In planning for children in care, the local authority should give first consideration to the need to safeguard and promote the welfare of the child throughout his or her childhood.

• There must be an assessment of children's needs and then an assessment of whether birth parents or parent substitutes could meet them and what assistance they would require.

• The local authority was prepared to help parents and children separate permanently when it was clear that they had no future together.

Key themes were the use of time limits and helping parents to understand and focus on the needs of their children and how to meet them.

In 1982, as a prelude to producing the training pack *In Touch with Parents* (Adcock and White, 1984), BAAF organised a small interdisciplinary seminar entitled 'Can we assess good enough parenting and, if so, how?' Three key ideas emerged (Adcock and White, 1985):

• Assessment needs to be done with and not to a family if some common agreement is to be reached about the nature of the problems that need resolution. Differing perceptions of problems do not constitute a helpful basis for planning work to achieve change.

• It was important that time was spent initially with families to get their agreement to participate in the process and to give them some idea of what is involved. Without this it might be difficult to assess their willingness and ability to work towards change.

• The processes of an assessment and the criteria used need to be shared with parents.

Morrison (1987) described a therapeutic assessment process to make decisions about rehabilitation. He said the task of the worker was an assessment of the parents and their capacity for change. In the final decision-making, key questions were the degree to which the professional team understood the family and how far the family understood itself, and to what extent the family had changed in the assessment process.

However, what was still lacking was a good research base showing which factors suggested the likelihood of rehabilitation and how this could be achieved with the minimum of damage to children.

Two articles from the USA provided this. Katz (1990) described concurrent planning, an assessment and decision-making scheme whereby children whose history suggested a very high probability of subsequent adoption were placed with foster carers who were also approved to adopt. The possibility of returning home and adoption were worked on concurrently not sequentially. Time limits for decision-making protected the child's development and a compulsory legal framework helped to activate/motivate the parents.

In a second article, Katz and Robinson (1991) discussed the parental assessment and decision-making that was based on research evidence about the likelihood of rehabilitation from a UK child psychiatrist, David Jones (1987). Conditions commonly encountered in the parents of children entering care were identified. Category 1 described five conditions so serious that any one being found would make family reunification very unlikely. Category 2 described 16 conditions that were less extreme but still strong contra-indicators for reunification. The more factors present, the more guarded the prognosis. Following the assessment, the parent(s) were offered intensive services to facilitate change within a time-limited period. In the previous four years about seven per cent of children accepted to the programme had been returned to birth parents. The others were adopted.

Katz spoke at several conferences in the UK, including one organised by BAAF in 1995. In 1999, the first concurrent planning project was established by Manchester Adoption Society, soon followed by Coram in London and then three local authorities.

Despite the good evidential base, however, concurrent planning has not become firmly established in the UK and three of the five projects have already closed. Financial difficulties, uncertainty on the part of social workers and human rights objections from lawyers all seem to have been contributory factors.

Conclusion
Assessment practice has evolved around a recognition that, at its heart, there is a relationship between the agency, the assessing social worker and the prospective carers, the child and the parents.

Within that relationship, adults and children can be helped to learn, understand, change and develop more positive and satisfying patterns of interaction. The extent to which this key relationship has become embedded in and drives assessment practice is questionable. It is a costly, time-consuming and skilled task. The danger is that in the current economic climate there will be increasing pressure to resort to greater use of 'scientific' tools and standardised assessments, and ignore the evidence that children and adults change and flourish within a positive and ongoing relationship with the agency where it models what is core to best practice in family placement. We need to reassert vigorously the core principles established through many years of practice to ensure that these 'life-changing' processes in family placement are driven by what we have learnt, know and understand.

References
Adcock M and White R (eds), *In Touch with Parents: Training materials for working with natural parents*, London: BAAF, 1984

Adcock M and White R (eds), *Good Enough Parenting: A framework for assessment*, London: BAAF, 1985

Bailey N and Batty D (eds), *In Touch with Children: Training materials on working with children*, London: BAAF, 1984

Barker S, Byrne S, Morrison M and Spencer M, *Making Good Assessments: A practical resource guide*, London: BAAF, 1999

Barth R and Berry M, *Adoption and Disruption: Rates, risks and responses*, Hawthorne, NY: Aldine de Gruyter, 1988

Chapman R, *Undertaking Fostering Assessments*, London: BAAF, 2009

Cousins J, *Pushing the Boundaries of Assessment*, London: BAAF, 2010

Dance C, Ouwejan D, Beecham J and Farmer E, *Linking and Matching: A survey of adoption agency practice in England and Wales*, London: BAAF, 2010

Davis S, Morris B and Thorn J, 'Task-centred assessment for foster parents', *Adoption & Fostering* 8:4, pp 33–37, 1984

Dibben E, *Undertaking an Adoption Assessment*, London: BAAF, 2010

Donley K, *Opening New Doors*, London: ABAFA, 1975

Fahlberg V, 'The child who is stuck', in Adcock M and White R (eds), *In Touch with Parents: Training materials for working with natural parents*, London: BAAF, 1984

Howe D, *Patterns of Adoption*, Oxford: Blackwell, 1998

Jones DP, 'The untreatable family', *Child Abuse and Neglect* 11:3 , pp 409–20, 1987

Jones DP, 'The effectiveness of intervention', in Adcock M and White R (eds), *Significant Harm*, Croydon: Significant Publications, 1998

Katz L, 'Effective permanency planning for children in foster care', *Social Work* 35:3, pp 220–26, 1990

Katz L and Robinson C, 'Foster care drift: a risk assessment matrix', *Child Welfare* 70:3, pp 347–58, 1991

Kellmer Pringle M, 'In place of one's own: looking beyond research', in ABAFA (ed), *Child Adoption: A selection of articles on adoption theory and practice*, London: ABAFA, 1976

Kirk DH, *Shared Fate: A theory and method of adoptive relationships*, Brentwood Bay, BC: Ben-Simon Publications, 1964 (revised 1984)

Lindsay Smith C, 'The New Families Project', in Triseliotis J (ed), *New Developments in Foster Care and Adoption*, London: Routledge & Kegan Paul, 1980

McKay M, 'Planning for permanent placement', *Adoption & Fostering* 99:1, pp 19–21, 1980

Morrison T, 'Creating change in abusing families', *Adoption & Fostering* 11:2, pp 25–29, 1987

Ruber M, 'New ABAFA form', *Adoption & Fostering* 90:4, p 7, 1977

Sawbridge P, 'Seeking new parents; a decade of development', Triseliotis J (ed), *New Developments in Foster Care and Adoption*, London: Routledge & Kegan Paul, 1980

Selwyn J, Sturgess W, Quinton D and Baxter C, *Costs and Outcomes of Non-infant Adoptions*, London: BAAF, 2006

Steele M, Hodges J, Kaniuk J, Hillman S and Henderson K, 'Attachment representations and adoption: associations between maternal states of mind and emotion narratives in previously maltreated children', *Journal of Child Psychotherapy* 29:2, pp 187–205, 2003

The law relating to adoption and fostering in England and Wales The contribution of BAAF

Richard White summarises BAAF's considerable influence on the development of child care law in England and Wales, from the Children Act 1975 and Adoption Act 1976 through to the Adoption and Children Act 2002.

Richard White is a Consultant Solicitor with McMillan Williams, and former Research Director and member of the BAAF Legal Group

Key words: child care law, BAAF, UK

Introduction

The placement of children away from their parents, whether in care or for adoption, can only take place in accordance with legal provisions, so it can be no surprise that BAAF has played a significant role in the development of child law. There have been two great eras of legal change in the lifetime of BAAF. These led to the Children Act 1989 and the Adoption and Children Act 2002. Both involved BAAF in years of thinking and debate and interaction with government. BAAF and its predecessors were enormously fortunate to have had on their permanent staff throughout these times two of the leading legal thinkers on the law relating to children. Solicitors Diana Rawstron, Deborah Cullen and now Alexandra Conroy Harris have ensured an expert legal presence and a continuity of thinking throughout a period of great development in the law. Furthermore, they have provided the ability to have published the important judicial decisions on child care law in *Adoption & Fostering*. Many of the leading practitioners and commentators, such as Queen's Counsel, Anita Ryan and Allan Levy, and Professors of Law, Nigel Lowe and Judith Masson, were all closely associated with the BAAF Legal Group; solicitors David Clark, Michael Sherwin and Richard White all first met at BAAF.

While this article is primarily focused on the last 30 years, it would be wrong to ignore the long-term impact of the Association of British Adoption Agencies (ABAA), previously the Standing Conference of Societies registered for Adoption, and later the Association of British Adoption and Fostering Agencies (ABAFA). They made a major contribution to the seminal report of the Houghton Committee published in October 1972. That report addressed many of the recurring issues in child placement, set out principles for a generation and bears reading now. In October 1973, ABAA published Rowe and Lambert's equally seminal *Children who Wait* (1973). The publications provided the foundation of the development of adoption law through changes in the Children Act 1975 and the Adoption Act 1976.

The 1970s were well known for recognising the importance of the protection of children against all forms of abuse but the need to plan for what happened if they had to be removed from their birth family permanently was not forgotten in legislation. Freeing for adoption was introduced in the 1975 Act, so that local authorities could plan for placement. Also introduced was the ill-fated, hardly used (much criticised by BAAF) and short-lived concept of custodianship, not implemented until 1985, repealed in 1991 and ultimately better provided for by special guardianship in the 2002 Act.

An examination of those, including the ABAA, who gave evidence to the Houghton Committee (1972), demonstrated its interdisciplinary context. This set the tone for the method of consultation which led to the momentous changes in the Children Act 1989 as a result of discussions through the 1980s. Although the 1989 Act excluded consideration of adoption law in detail, its relationship to the mainstream of child law was implanted.

The Children Act years

The many disparate statutory provisions and varying powers at different levels of the court system necessitated a comprehensive review of the system. The fundamental work of the 1980s was the *Review of Child Care Law* (Department of Health and Social Security, 1985), set up in response to a recommendation from the House of Commons Social Services Committee in 1983. The Review reported to ministers following a seminar to which many of those interested in child law were invited and had sent written contributions, including BAAF. This was a vital stage in the progress towards the Children Act 1989.

The 1989 Act covered virtually all the law relating to the care and upbringing of children and the services provided in support, save for adoption and youth crime. It was considered to be the most comprehensive and far-reaching reform of this branch of the law ever introduced.

Prior to the 1989 Act there were provisions in the Children Act 1948, which empowered local authorities to acquire what were then parental rights and duties in respect of children who had been placed in care without recourse to court. BAAF set up a research project to consider the history of those children and made recommendations that local authorities should have to apply to the court. This was later incorporated in the 1989 Act.

What the research also demonstrated was the lack of planning for children in care, in spite of the provisions introduced in the 1975 Act, both in terms of placement and the arbitrary arrangements for children to have contact with their birth families. The interests of some of those children necessitated closer management of the child's relationship with the birth family. The permanence philosophy developed from this thinking. Also significant was the decision in *Re F* [1982] 1 WLR 102 in which the Court of Appeal emphasised the importance of the stability of adoption as opposed to long-term fostering.

BAAF held a seminar for professionals that led to the publication of *Terminating Parental Contact: An exploration of the issues in relation to children in care* (Adcock and White, 1979). Some authorities became vigorous in stopping contact and in *A v Liverpool City Council* [1982] AC 363 the House of Lords confirmed that that decision was within their powers. As a result, provisions were introduced in the Health and Social Security and Social Services Act 1983, which gave parents a right of appeal to the then juvenile court and required authorities to act in accordance with a Code of Practice on Access.

Contemporaneously, greater attention was given to the possibility of the making of adoption orders even though a parent was unwilling to consent. Although the provisions for dispensing with consent had existed in the Adoption Act 1958 and the House of Lords, in the landmark decisions in *Re W (An Infant)* [1971] AC 682 and in *O'Connor v A and B* [1971] 2 All ER 1230, had given a wide interpretation to the grounds, practice did not develop as fast as the law. In *O'Connor* it was said:

The instability of the natural parents and the disruption which may be caused by removal of a child who had been in the care of the adopters for two-and-a half-years were reasons for not interfering with the decision [to make an adoption order].

Yet cases of adoption orders opposed by parents remained rare. It needed a change in social work practice to produce stability for children.

Family Justice: A structure for the family court was published by BAAF in 1986 and set out arguments for a unified jurisdiction for family justice. It was the product of a BAAF Working Party chaired by Denis Allen, an influential Director of Social Services. Its thinking, while not fully implemented by a unified court, was reflected in one principle of the 1989 Act that there should be easy links between each level of the court system and that they should have broadly the same powers.

In 1984, another in the BAAF Discussion Series, *Taking a Stand*, was developed from an interdisciplinary seminar. One of a number of leading child psychiatrists at the seminar, Dr Stephen Wolkind wrote about the skills of assessing a child's needs measured against wider clinical experience based on a body of scientific and theoretical knowledge. This event marked an important development in the conduct and management of complex child proceedings. Regrettably, however, it later led to over-complication and a tendency to use such evidence only in proceedings rather than ensuring that it was widely available for reaching decisions about a range of children who were not the subject of proceedings. Latterly, the involvement of medical and psychological experts has been seen to undermine the willingness of courts to accept expert evidence from other disciplines and has led to delays in the conduct of proceedings.

What emerged clearly from these years, and was fundamental to the ethos of the 1989 Act, was the importance of ensuring that in care proceedings parents had legal representation and fair notice of decisions and an impartial tribunal to consider the case with independent legal and social work qualified representation of the child. All of those considerations are important to keep in mind when we are entering an era in which memories of those days are fading and Ministry of Justice thinking is contemplating moving those powers away from the courts.

One small but significant amendment in the 1989 legislation was the provision for adoption proceedings to be regarded as family proceedings. It made it possible for other family orders to be made on an application for adoption. While this was unlikely – and could be regarded as a potential undermining of the unique concept of adoption – it had the advantage of relating it to the mainstream of child law.

The Adoption Act years

When the dust settled on the 1989 Act thought turned to adoption and the need for updating that legislation, and how it should become part of a comprehensive system of child law. As with the 1989 Act, the Adoption and Children Act 2002 was long in its development and comprehensive and far-reaching in its scope. Work continued over many years following the publication of *Adoption: The Future* by the Department of Health (1993).

BAAF lobbied hard throughout the 1990s for adoption work to be brought into the mainstream of local authority thinking but it was not until 1999, when the Department of Health published *Adoption Now: Messages from research*, that government thinking started to become focused. John Hutton, then Minister at the Department, wrote in his foreword: 'we are determined . . . to ensure that adoption becomes part of the mainstream of these services [for children]'.

There were distractions from the core need for stability for children. While many of the areas of development in the law were largely a matter of debating how to reflect in statutory provisions complex social issues, there were also major conflicts. These can perhaps be grouped as follows:

• the extent to which adoption was the status of choice for children who could not live with their birth family or whether some other form of legal order was to be preferred, especially in the placement of older children who might have had a significant albeit traumatic relationship with parents (which led to special guardianship);

• supplementary to that, whether and, if so, what form of contact was desirable;

• supplementary to that, what information should be disclosed about the child and the adoption placement;

• the extent of disclosure of historical information about an adopted child;

• whether placement of children with adopters of a different 'race' or ethnicity could be in their interests;

- whether same-sex couples should be approved to adopt, and if so whether placements with them would be limited to children with special needs who were harder to place.

Focus on the identity of the birth family and sometimes the 'rights' of the parents was for some time thought to necessitate face-to-face contact. While that might still remain the case for some children and with some parents, BAAF worked out that later access to birth records and exchange of information between the birth and adoptive families might often provide best for the future needs of the adopted child.

Delay in Adoption Proceedings, a report by the President's Adoption Committee, was published in May 2000 and made an important contribution to speeding up the judicial process of adoption proceedings and later to the structure of the 2002 Act. BAAF's then Chief Executive, Felicity Collier, and Deborah Cullen and David Clark were members of that committee. The provision of adoption centres with judges experienced in adoption work was of major importance.

In July 2000, the Government published the *Prime Minister's Review of Adoption* (Performance and Innovation Unit, 2000) which gave the necessary impetus to the new legislation.

The future

Some parts of government have long been critical of what they regard as the Rolls Royce services which a time of promoting the interests of children and their rights, health and well-being brought about in care, education and self-determination. The recession has created an opportunity for that to be reassessed and there are serious concerns that children's services will deteriorate.

There are still regularly new legal issues to consider; as the last 30 years has illustrated, there has to be constant renewal. To name but a few in a deteriorating social system and a move away from a family justice system, one can anticipate a need to consider the law relating to thresholds for care and support services, the nature of the family justice system, its boundaries with the respective powers of the courts and local authorities and their interaction, post-adoption and post-placement services, and artificial parenting and reproduction law (with its many issues comparable with adoption).

At a time when private legal practice in family law is under such threat, BAAF will need to ensure that it retains its focus on legal development.

References

Adcock M and White RAH (eds), *Terminating Parental Contact: An exploration of the issues relating to children in care*, London: BAAF, 1979

BAAF, *Taking a Stand: Child psychiatrists in custody, access and disputed adoption cases*, Discussion Series 5, London: BAAF, 1984

BAAF/ADSS, *Family Justice: A structure for the family court*, London: BAAF, 1986

Department of Health, *Adoption: The Future*, Cm 2288, London: HMSO, 1993

Department of Health, *Adoption Now: Messages from research*, Chichester: John Wiley & Sons, 1999

Department of Health and Social Security, *Review of Child Care Law: Report to Ministers of an Interdepartmental Working Party*, London: The Stationery Office, 1985

The Houghton Committee, *Departmental Committee Report on the Adoption of Children*, Cmnd. 5107, London: HMSO, 1972

Performance and Innovation Unit, *Prime Minister's Review of Adoption*, London: The Cabinet Office, 2000

President's Adoption Committee, *Delay in Adoption Proceedings*, London: Lord Chancellor's Department, 2000

Rowe J and Lambert L, *Children who Wait*, London: ABAA, 1973

Doctors and nurses in advance of their time
The BAAF Health Advisory Group

Mary Mather celebrates BAAF's pioneering role in placing health care at the heart of social care practice with children separated from their birth parents. In particular, the contribution of the Health Group, for example re-evaluating assessment procedures, promoting training and education, and supporting designated doctors and nurses, is discussed.

Mary Mather is a Consultant Paediatrician and former Chair of the BAAF Health Group (2003–2008)

Key words: BAAF Health Group, re-evaluating assessment, designated doctors and nurses, health of looked after children

We only found out that his mother was epileptic after his first fit. They also forgot to mention that his mother could not read or write. We feel so guilty; we wasted all those years in school.
(Adopters of a seven-year-old boy)

Introduction

When health is ignored or marginalised in care planning, families and children often pay a very heavy price. Adoption and fostering are principally social services; however, they contain within them a small but very important health component. Without the support of BAAF, this health component might have been largely forgotten. BAAF should be justly proud of the role it has played in advocating for better health for the most disadvantaged children in society and in promoting the role of the health professionals who care for them. Most European and US adoption and fostering agencies, whether state or voluntary, have never experienced the direct involvement of health care practitioners at the heart of their social care practice.

It was the pioneering vision of BAAF, rather than the demands of legislation or the dictates of professional organisations, that first brought health and social care together and over 30 years has created an exceptional working partnership. The BAAF Health Group (formerly Medical Group) appears to be unique. Ahead of its time and outside the mainstream concerns of the health professions, doctors and nurses, together with BAAF employees, have tirelessly advocated for the health and well-being of children requiring substitute care.

Some history

The original Medical Group was formed in 1964 and is therefore considerably older than BAAF itself. Those who think that excellence, quality and the pursuit of standards in clinical practice are a recent phenomenon will find an afternoon spent among the dusty files of the BAAF archives very instructive. Over 50 years ago, a small group of dedicated medical advisers, who were extremely concerned about the differing standards of medical practice across the voluntary agencies then involved in adoption work, decided to work together as a group. They spent most of their early meetings designing and redesigning medical forms to ensure overall consistency of practice, an unending exercise that still taxes and exasperates the present Health Group. However, there is no doubt that the BAAF forms, now used by most local authorities and voluntary agencies, provide the template for an achievable, sustainable, high-quality, holistic health assessment. Clinical governance, the buzz word of the 1990s, merely requires professionals to implement what medical advisers and BAAF sought to achieve 30 years earlier.

Adoption first became legal in the UK in 1926 and for the next 50 years adoption practice was primarily about finding white healthy babies for white, married, affluent childless couples. The medical input to adoption was minimal. Newborn babies were given a brief physical examination to exclude major health problems or congenital malformations. Children unlucky enough to have any medical problems, even minor ones, were likely to be labelled as unadoptable and not placed. The health needs of children requiring other types of permanent care, most of whom would be placed in local authority nurseries or foster homes, were largely forgotten until the pioneering publication of *Children who Wait* by Jane Rowe and Lydia Lambert (1973).

Over the next two decades, as the number of babies looking for adoptive families decreased, substitute care became increasingly seen as the best option for children whose parents were unable, unwilling or judged by the legal system as unfit to care for them. Many of these children had complex physical, developmental, emotional and educational needs. They were likely to be damaged by inadequate parenting, drug misuse or neglect. They were more likely to be older, looking for placements with their siblings and from a variety of ethnic backgrounds. Social work practice and the medical skill and experience needed to support the substitute care of children therefore changed dramatically and the BAAF Health Group was always at the forefront, leading the necessary changes in practice.

A radical review of assessment

The health of children separated from their parents is always vulnerable. Despite a raft of government initiatives over the last 15 years, looked after children remain among the most disadvantaged children in British society. The majority become looked after as a consequence of neglect and abuse, either before birth, during early childhood or both. Bringing a child into the care system should ideally lead to improved long-term health and well-being. Sadly, for many children the exact opposite is still the case.

In 1997, the Health Group was the first to point out that looked after children did not have a high priority in strategic planning for health, education or social services. As far as health was concerned, research into their needs was very limited and publications thin on the ground, even in dedicated journals. There was emerging evidence to suggest that health care failed most of the children and the services which were

offered to them were undervalued and often rejected (Butler and Payne, 1997; Mather *et al*, 1997).

Subsequent research has overwhelmingly indicated that, compared to children of the same age and social status who live with their birth parents, looked after children are known to have incomplete immunisations, lower child health surveillance uptake rates, worse dental health, poorer nutrition and more unhealthy lifestyles. They also suffer school failure, which affects their adult health. They have more behavioural problems and mental health disorders, especially depression, attention deficit hyperactivity disorder and post-traumatic stress disorder. As adults they have higher rates of teenage pregnancy, smoking, alcohol or drug misuse, homelessness, unemployment and imprisonment.

The Health Group was also the first to realise that assessments done on looked after children needed to be more than physical examinations. Children with this degree of disadvantage needed something completely different; they needed 'health assessments'. Although this includes a physical examination, children with incomplete immunisations, untested hearing and vision, developmental delay, emotional difficulties and incomplete or missing records needed something more. They needed a holistic review of their physical, developmental, emotional and social health.

The assessment of child health is a complex process that requires training, support, interagency working and resources. Uniquely, the Health Group has also always been adamant that there must be no variation between the assessments offered to children going to the potential security of adoption and those who remain in state care throughout their childhood.

The Health Group has argued from the beginning that the comprehensive assessment of a child will facilitate a placement rather than threaten its stability. For many years, however, there was a reluctance on the part of social workers to highlight concerns precisely for fear of delaying a placement or deterring carers. It is fascinating that a very robust discussion was minuted over 30 years ago, when medical advisers had a vigorous debate about when the adoption medical should be done. In those early days, some were being carried out after placement and children were being returned by their potential adopters when problems were uncovered. The Medical Group Executive Committee was emphatic that this was not only bad for the child and family but was a totally unethical practice. They were adamant that medicals and reports always came first and strongly advised their members to have no part in poor practice. However, it took many years before it was widely recognised that what substitute carers require is a very honest assessment of the difficulties they are likely to face in the future.

Mental health issues have a similar history. There is currently a much-needed focus on the mental health needs of children in general and looked after children in particular, but for many years there was a reluctance to engage in discussion with substitute carers about these issues. Against this background, the Group Executive Committee insisted on adding annexes to the BAAF forms which concentrated on emotional health, behaviour and educational support. These forms were the first systematic attempt to look at the mental health of children in the care system. They were introduced at a time when child mental health was rarely considered as a placement issue. The HIV and hepatitis B and C testing of looked after children has a similar history. With hindsight, these moves were very much ahead of their time but were frequently unpopular with our colleagues in social services. Thankfully we have all moved on together.

The role of designated doctors and nurses

Quality Protects (Department of Health, 1998) introduced the concept of designated doctors and nurses for looked after children and there are now more than 100 such nurses in post across the country. Designated nurses are effective and successful; they can reach the isolated, alienated vulnerable child in a way which is difficult for a doctor working from a conventional clinic or consulting room. They are particularly effective in building relationships with teenagers and older children, the group most likely to refuse to see a doctor.

In 2003, after a national consultation, as the contribution made by nurses was recognised and the value of them being able to stand for election to the group in their own right was acknowledged, the name of the BAAF Medical Group was changed to the BAAF Health Group. The name change also recognised that there are many other professional groups involved in the health care of looked after children. The decision to alter the name was a bold one, expressing a belief in the uniqueness of the individual child and the importance of securing health for all children, not just those fortunate enough to grow up in the care of their parents. Hopefully in the future, it will be possible to welcome child psychiatrists, clinical psychologists, public health specialists, dentists, dieticians and general practitioners as full members.

Health services for looked after children also depend on the availability of a skilled, well-trained and dedicated workforce. If in the past, the needs of the children have been neglected by society, so too have the professional and developmental needs of doctors and nurses who care for them. The work can be isolating. In any primary care trust or district, there is usually only one doctor or nurse engaged in adoption and fostering work experiencing the problems of isolation, lack of support and markedly different expectations from region to region.

The competencies of the medical practitioner working as the lead doctor for looked after children must be broad. They must include the ability to assess a child where there is little medical information and where family medical and genetic histories may be missing.

They need specialised knowledge of consent and confidentiality in situations of complex parental responsibility. Knowledge of child mental health, specifically attachment disorders and post-traumatic stress disorder, is essential. Doctors must be able to assess infants in situations where the long-term outcome may be difficult to predict, such as extreme prematurity or exposure to drugs and alcohol in pregnancy. Paediatricians often struggle with advice on adult health issues. For example, what are the long-term implications for a child whose birth parents have mental health problems? This is a unique situation in paediatric practice. They need an ability to liaise and communicate effectively with colleagues in a multi-agency setting and a capacity to express complex medical issues in lay terms.

Promoting education and professional support

The Health Group, together with BAAF, has over the years produced a number of very useful publications and practice notes. These have included a major publication on children exposed to substance misuse (Phillips, 2004) and guidance on using the BAAF health assessment forms (2004b), the health screening of children adopted from abroad (2004a), the genetic testing of children (2006) and testing for blood-borne viruses (2008). They were the first group to point out the dangers of exposing children to passive cigarette smoke (2007) and guidance on obesity in carers is hot off the press (Mather and Lehrner, 2010). The only UK textbooks for medical advisers were published by BAAF (Mather and Batty, 2000; Millar and Fursland, 2006).

Continuing education and professional development are essential if professional standards are to be maintained. The education of doctors and nurses involved in substitute care is probably unique in that for 30 years it has been largely undertaken by BAAF. There cannot be another area of medical practice in which the voluntary sector, as opposed to professional organisations, has been

so responsible for training. Membership of the BAAF Health Group is still the only forum that offers professional support, training opportunities, updates on policy and practice and access to national and regional meetings. The tradition of continuing education is also maintained in the form of the Annual General Meeting of the Health Group. Doctors and nurses in increasing numbers from all over the country meet to discuss new developments in practice, shared problems and future developments. The group also contributes regularly to the Health Notes section of *Adoption & Fostering* and edited a special edition devoted to health (Mather, 2002).

The presence of a support group which meets regularly for discussion and training is invaluable to the isolated professional. The BAAF Health Group has a number of regional groups supported by their local regional offices. The dynamic contribution of these groups is of increasing importance. The Scottish Group was the first to be established as a formal sub-group in 1979 and since then, beginning with the north-west of England, informal groups have developed in Wales and all the other English regions. The Scottish and Welsh Groups in particular, given the differences in legislation following devolution, have played a major role in co-ordinating and leading on health policy and training.

Advocacy has always been recognised as important to doctors involved in substitute care. Initially, many medical advisers lacked the status or inclination to make an impact, but now with the expectation that they will be recruited from the ranks of senior paediatricians, this task has become easier.

The importance of the role of the medical adviser was only slowly recognised by our fellow paediatricians. Adoption and fostering has at last appeared on the course syllabus for the training of specialist registrars in paediatrics. Competencies in this area are being developed with colleagues from the Royal College of Paediatrics and Child Health. The challenge of the future is to ensure that the quality of practice is maintained as the mechanism for commissioning health services changes yet again.

Concluding thoughts

Looking back over the last 30 years, the Health Group has much to be proud of although many challenges lie ahead. Despite the expenditure of large amounts of public money, eleven per cent of looked after children will still have more than three foster placements in any year. Any failure to achieve placement stability has major consequences for health. Many children are lost to health follow-up when they move out of an area. There is a general shortage of information technology and administrative support, which is an essential back-up for children who move placements frequently. The child's social worker can change very frequently. Multiple moves often mean different general practitioners, arguments about funding, missing records, lack of family history, no obstetric history, absent developmental histories and missing immunisation records. Medical examinations can still be isolated events carried out by several different doctors. Above all, the goal of good health outcomes for every looked after child still remains elusive.

The medical input to substitute care still needs to be put firmly on the agenda of mainstream paediatric practice. Resources remain a major issue. In many paediatric services adoption and fostering are sidelined, poorly resourced and the training needs of the doctors and nurses in the service neglected. Many of the nursing posts are only funded in the short term and may fall victim to public sector cuts. Parental substance misuse is a sizeable and escalating problem that is having a serious and unpredictable impact on children and their carers.

Thousands of children have benefited from the generosity and commitment of their substitute parents and the vision of the BAAF. The opportunity to give a child a second chance is rare. The resources and support generously given to health within BAAF has given generations of doctors and nurses the training and professional development to deliver a better service to children who have few advocates. On their behalf, we offer our thanks, our congratulations and our sincere hope that the association continues in the future.

References

BAAF, 'Health screening of children adopted from abroad', *Practice Note* 46, London: BAAF, 2004

BAAF, 'Using the BAAF health assessment forms', *Practice Note* 47, London: BAAF, 2004

BAAF, 'Genetic testing and adoption', *Practice Note* 50, London: BAAF, 2006

BAAF, 'Reducing the risks of environmental tobacco smoke for looked after children and their carers', *Practice Note* 51, London: BAAF, 2007

BAAF, 'Guidelines for the testing of looked after children who are at risk of a bloodborne infection', *Practice Note* 53, London: BAAF, 2008

Butler I and Payne H, 'The health of children looked after by the local authority', *Adoption & Fostering* 21:2, pp 28–35, 1997

Department of Health, *Quality Protects: Transforming children's services – objectives for social services and children*, London: HMSO, 1998

Mather M (ed), *Promoting children's health*, Special issue, *Adoption & Fostering* 26:4, 2002

Mather M and Batty D, *Doctors for Children in Public Care*, London: BAAF, 2000

Mather M and Lehrner K, *Evaluating Obesity in Substitute Carers*, London: BAAF, 2010

Mather M, Humphrey J and Robson J, 'The statutory medical and health needs of looked after children', *Adoption & Fostering* 21:2, pp 36–40, 1997

Millar I with Fursland E, *A Guide for Medical Advisers: Advocating, promoting and protecting the health of looked after children in Scotland*, London: BAAF, 2006

Phillips R (ed), *Children Exposed to Parental Substance Misuse*, London: BAAF, 2004

Rowe J and Lambert L, *Children who Wait*, London: ABAFA, 1973

Contact between looked after children and their parents A level playing field?

Contact between looked after children and their parents has assumed in recent years a much higher profile than ever before, as have judgements about its merits. Important decisions regarding the continuation of contact and the granting of care, placement or adoption orders now rely heavily on evidence of its likely benefits to the child. Yet, as **John Triseliotis** asserts in this article, there is a dearth of empirically-based theory and of agreed criteria and guidelines when making judgements about whether there should be any contact at all, its frequency and the assessment of its quality.

John Triseliotis is Emeritus Professor at the University of Edinburgh and a Child Placement Consultant

Key words:
assessment, contact, looked after children

Introduction

Over the last 20 years, the quality of contact between children absent in care and their parents has assumed a much higher profile than ever before. Those supervising contact are now expected to keep records on meetings and report on their quality to reviews, courts and, in Scotland, children's panels. When courts are requested to grant a care, placement or an adoption order, a key question almost always asked is the quality of contact. Depending on the evidence, direct contact may be provided for, reduced or stopped altogether.

Yet judgements on the quality of contact lack a coherent and empirically based theory and guidelines. The recent ascendancy of attachment theory has offered a kind of framework of what to look for, but important as Bowlby's (1969) theory is, there is much more to parenthood and child development than attachments. John Sutherland, former Director of the Tavistock Clinic, co-founder of the Scottish Institute of Human Relations and a close acquaintance of Bowlby, wrote that 'the attachment phenomena are very real, but I do not think these terms are adequate for the ongoing inner processes' (see Scharff, 2007, p 171).

The introduction of direct contact after adoption in a few selected cases and contact between non-resident parents and children following divorce or separation have raised awareness of the importance of contact and led to a number of studies. However, the details surrounding the subject, which affects thousands of children each year, remain under researched.

Making judgements on the quality and nature of contact remains a mixture of art and science, possibly balanced more towards art. On the whole, there are no empirically-based guidelines or standardised tests on what to look for and no criteria for evaluating events during meetings. There is also no script for parents on how to conduct themselves, what to do and not do, what to say and not say, and no guidelines for those supervising meetings on how to assess what they observe. The often used Family Relations exercise does not seem to transfer well from the US and has to be adapted. Once this happens, however, it ceases to be standardised. Ticking boxes on forms, as another method, begs the question regarding the accuracy of the perceptions and their interpretation. Yet parents who attend supervised meetings have a right to know on what kind of criteria they are being judged, how these have been arrived at and how reliable they are. When the issue of contact after adoption emerged as an important variable in decision-making around the late 1980s, Triseliotis (1991) set out tentative criteria of what might be looked for. However, recognising these qualities and their strength still remains a problem.

Compared to the thousands of children who are looked after in care, contact after adoption is much rarer and usually comes at the tail end of a child's life in care. But what happens with contact beforehand often determines and pre-empts decisions about rehabilitation or permanence outside the birth family, so radically affecting children's lives.

Promoting contact

Child care legislation across the UK places a responsibility on local authorities not only to encourage contact between children in care and their families, but also 'to promote' it whenever it is consistent with the child's welfare. It looks upon this as a 'right' of the child and not of the parent or other birth relative. Besides encouraging, supporting and making enabling arrangements, the 'promotion' of contact would also imply preparing parents and explaining why their visits are important to their children, how they might use contact more productively and how they would be judged. But no preparatory arrangements appear to exist, suggesting that had parents known beforehand how to positively engage, play and stimulate their children, some of their offspring might not have been in care.

The changes in the legislation came about mainly after early studies identified the difficulties experienced by many birth parents when trying to visit their children. For instance, poor organisation, discouraging attitudes and long distances between placements and home communities presented them with significant logistic transport problems and expenses. Millham *et al* (1986) reported that many parents of children in foster and residential care felt unwanted and believed they had nothing more to contribute to the well-being of their children once they were away from home. While most barriers to contact were informal and non-specific, others were ordered by the courts – balancing the wishes of children and families, supervision, timing and venue. More recent studies have noted improved practices, including higher levels of commitment on the part of social workers and foster carers, children increasingly being placed nearer their home communities, easier travel arrangements for parents and the use of venues with better play and other facilities (Cleaver, 1997/8, 2000;

Triseliotis *et al*, 2000). However, there are still examples of contact being viewed as if it were arranged for the benefit of parents and continuing obstacles occur. How else to explain why a meeting is cancelled due to a parent who had to negotiate public transport arriving a few minutes late, with the child being left high and dry as the parent leaves after being denied access? Or when contact is arranged at a distant venue, difficult to reach by public transport, to 'test' a parent's motivation? When a parent misses a meeting, it is rightly condemned for the distress this causes to the child and is rarely rearranged, but a quite different view is taken when the escort or supervising worker suddenly withdraws.

The claimed benefits of contact to children

Contact is a difficult and highly emotive experience for both children and parents and there are no easy or definitive answers. In spite of increased studies, there is still much to be learnt about whom it is for, its purpose, how to organise it, where it should take place, how to interpret what occurs during meetings, how to make reliable judgements about it and whether it benefits a particular child. Howe and Steele (2004) assert the presence of 'strong evidence' pointing to how children benefit from contact, including many who had suffered maltreatment – although they acknowledge that in a 'few exceptional cases' contact would be ill advised due to the effects of previous abuse or risk of recurrence. They cite Weinstein's (1960) pioneering study which demonstrated how children who were visited were more likely to return home earlier and have a better self-image than those who were not. Equally important was Trasler's (1960) finding that a lack of knowledge of what is happening to their families and themselves 'creates severe anxiety' in foster children, which is then reflected in their behaviour. Other studies relate continuing positive contact for children to fewer fostering breakdowns and better adjustment (Holman,

1973; Berridge and Cleaver, 1987; Thoburn and Rowe, 1988; Wedge and Mantle, 1991). Further benefits identified include: the strengthening of genealogical and physical identity; reassuring the child that the birth parent is well and continues to care; helping to assuage anxiety and possible guilt; demonstrating love and affection; reducing feelings of loss and rejection; promoting a positive sense of self; and helping to avoid fantasising (Weinstein, 1960; Hess and Proch, 1993; Hetherington and Stanley-Hagan, 1999; Neil and Howe, 2004; Smith and Logan, 2004).

These benefits are not guaranteed, as much depends on the individual child's past experiences, how parents use contact, their relationship with the child, their support for the placement and emotional sanctioning to the child to live there, the relationship between parents and carers and the absence of undermining attitudes and threatening behaviours. Therefore, saying that positive contact benefits looked after children begs the question of what is positive and how benefit is identified and quantified. These qualifications are especially salient for children who have been severely abused or neglected. However, Elizabeth Butler-Sloss, former President of the High Court Family Division, is reported to have said that:

Violent behaviour alone was not enough to deny a parent contact with a child. It would be for the court to decide, if violence had been proved, how relevant it was. (*The Times*, 10 November 2001)

Nevertheless, concerns remain; the psychotherapist Loxterkamp (2009) has raised the stakes by challenging the notion that post-adoption contact between children and birth relatives who have abused, maltreated or neglected them confers any benefits to the children. Whereas Howe and Steele (2004) carefully stress the need to consider this in 'a few exceptional' cases, Loxterkamp expands the categories of children to include neglect, maltreatment and abuse, without making qualifications about

severity and extent, leaving it understood that almost all contact is highly questionable. He appears to dismiss studies, for instance by Smith and Logan (2004), which demonstrate that in the right cases direct contact after adoption on the whole works well. While Loxterkamp is right to question the evidence, his broad categories of neglect, abuse and maltreatment apply to the majority of those entering care and so exclude them from qualifying for contact.

The frequency and duration of contact

There is a presumption in law that contact will be 'reasonable', but this is not defined and no study so far seems to have identified the appropriate frequency of contact for each group of looked after children. No doubt when arranging for frequency and duration, account has to be taken of the child's specific circumstances, age, needs, wishes if old enough, and the parent's ability to manage the frequency. In the event of permanency plans being introduced, and depending on their stability, contact may then be adjusted appropriately. However, any reduction has to be proportionate until the court makes its final decision, especially as the stability of some placements can be very unpredictable.

It is also recognised that after young children are accommodated and placed in foster care, their main closeness will be to their foster carers. As a result, any relationship developed with the birth parent(s) will rely on contact and its quality. Under such circumstances close or strong attachments to birth parents are unusual. Furthermore, the relationship and closeness of such a child to the birth parent can only be relative to that with his or her primary carer. This is especially so when the child has been accommodated from birth. What mostly happens when contact is positive is the development of strong familiarity and a relationship of some strength, together with a degree of emotional connectedness; but even with regular contact, as Katz *et al* (1994, p 23) point out, this is difficult to achieve if you are not the child's primary carer. Nevertheless, Weinstein (1960, p 69) stresses that it is wrong to conclude that if a child identifies predominantly with their foster carers, continuing contact with birth parents is not still very important to him or her.

While many practitioners are aware of these qualifications and take account of them when making evaluations on the quality of contact, others still judge the parents as if they were the child's primary carers. Comments such as 'no "strong" attachments exist', 'he does not react to his mother as a person who looks after him', 'when his female carer is present the child goes more often to her than to his mother', are not uncommon. Yet it is understandable that a young child who has been fostered from birth or when a few months old would react in this way, especially if contact is infrequent. In fact, if such a child did not display stronger attachments to his carer than to the visiting parent, questions would have to be asked about the quality of parenting provided. Despite this, the lack of strong emotional links between child and birth parent is likely to be used in court as a strong argument for stopping or drastically reducing contact.

Possibly the most contentious issue regarding contact and its frequency has to do with when it is justified to reduce or even stop it altogether and who makes that decision. Considering the thousands of children affected, research-based guidance is sparse and mainly comes from cases of divorce or separation, and more recently from studies in contact after adoption. For example, should the same criterion be used for stopping contact as that for the granting of a care order, namely that continuing contact is likely to cause more harm and distress? In Scotland decisions on the frequency, duration, reduction and stopping of contact are made by lay children's panels, on the recommendation of social workers. Parents may appeal to the court but by the time some cases are heard it can be too late. Furthermore, a finding in favour of the parent can later be reversed by the same panel, making a new appeal necessary, by which stage some parents give up. There is at times too much confrontation between parents and social workers; with some parents resorting to the internet and Facebook (see Fursland, 2010), it is time to move towards more conciliation – provided that contact continues to be in the child's interests.

Professional experiences and studies suggest that it is not at all unusual to blame contact when a child is unsettled before, during or after its occurrence, or is reluctant to attend. Monck et al (2003, p 187) reported from their study of concurrent placements that the children's carers were particularly sensitive to any signs of distress in the children, and had 'a tendency' to ascribe this to contact with birth parents. Even though there was no doubt that contact sessions were unsettling for a number of children, this may not have been a product of the contact per se but of the surrounding circumstances, such as long journeys, strange environments and disturbed routines.

There can be other explanations for why a child shows reluctance to attend contact meetings or displays unsettled behaviour before, during and afterwards. Who takes a young child to contact and how familiar she or he happens to be to the child could influence the child's reaction and attendance, especially given the high turnover of escort and supervising workers. The same applies to how the carer, on whom the child depends for their physical and emotional needs, prepares, supports and encourages him or her to attend. Exclusive carers may fail to convey the right messages and sufficient encouragement and support (Holman, 1980). Children are usually quick to pick up on a carer or resident parent's emotions; persistent anxiety or mistrust of contact on the part of the primary carer could lead the child to experience similar feelings and a loyalty conflict, and then refuse to attend or display distress. Similarly, a carer may be encouraging the child verbally to attend but emotionally indicate disapproval and disloyalty, so producing unsettled behaviour and pressures from carers on social workers and panels to stop contact (Wilkinson, 1988, p 236; Ames Reed, 1993; McCauley, 2002).

Separation anxiety from the primary carer, be it a foster carer or a prospective adopter, is not uncommon among young children. A child who does not yet feel secure enough may not trust that the carer will still be there on his or her return from contact. It is common for such children to engage well with the parent during contact and appear content, until the next meeting when the separation anxiety resurfaces. Once the child is satisfied that the primary carer will still be there on return, the anxiety usually fades away. As contact is such an emotive experience for both parent and child, it has to be expected that for a period of time afterwards the child may still be reacting to the engagement, irrespective of whether it was positive or negative. Sinclair (2005) noted that children usually look forward to contact, commonly want more contact than they get, but are nevertheless commonly upset by it – again, given the proviso that there will always be a few children who will be reluctant to take part in meetings from which they gain no benefit or that revive memories of past abuse (see Howe and Steele, 2004).

One explanation offered for the drastic reduction and sometimes stopping of contact is that the child does not talk to their carer and/or social worker about it, often interpreted as a sign of indifference. But, as Cleaver (2000, p 272) found, 'It was rare for children to make their views on contact known to either carers or social workers.'

Especially in the case of under-five-year-olds, drastically reducing or stopping contact – without evidence that it causes harm or distress or has the potential for doing so, but simply on account of permanency plans and before the case comes to court – inevitably weakens the emotional link between a young child and a parent. So at subsequent hearings, often one to two years later, parents who ask for contact are told that their emo-tional link or relationship with the child is weak or absent or that the child no longer asks for them.

A further argument for the drastic reduction or cessation of contact is that it will prevent the child from attaching to a new family. Loxterkamp (2009, p 425) writes:

The later adopted child will inevitably have strong feelings about members of the birth family and longings to be with some or many of them. These longings will interfere with the forming of secure relationships with the adoptive parents and family.

However, studies by Schaffer (1990), Fratter *et al* (1991) and Berridge (1997) all conclude that there is no evidence to support the view that continued contact with birth parents prevents children from becoming attached to new parents, other than in the minority of cases where original parents deliberately set out to wreck a placement. It seems that children are much more capable of sorting out the roles of the various individuals in their lives and sustaining relationships with all of them than they have been given credit for. Children mostly become muddled when the adults in their lives become confused and adversarial. This is not to deny the serious difficulties that poor-quality contact predicts disruption, and the problems that arise when birth relatives refuse to accept the situation and convey their emotional permission for the child to live with his or her new family and look upon new carers as parents.

Venue

Where children meet their parents for contact varies according to age, preference and level of risk. In a study of foster care, almost half of contact (44%) took place within the parental home, almost a third (30%) within the foster home, a similar proportion at the social work office/centre and 20 per cent elsewhere (Triseliotis *et al*, 2000). (The figures add up to more than 100 per cent as children saw their parents in several places.) Due to changing attitudes and the need to supervise and observe contact, including in situations of potential risk, it is likely that a much higher proportion of contact takes place now within family centres and social work locations. Young children mostly enjoy family centres, which provide appropriate toys and games. However, these are not very suitable for children over about the age of four who tend to prefer activity-type facilities, such as climbing frames, chutes and tunnels which are usually found in adventure centres, or like to go swimming, bowling or ice-skating. Although foster homes still have their place as venues, possibly for babies, they can make visiting parents feel anxious and tense; also, some parents may pose risks to the foster carers. Thus, in spite of much progress parents and children are often thrown back on their ingenuity while simultaneously being criticised for not being more inventive. It is not much fun for the parent and child having contact in an office, or in a storeroom cluttered with office furniture, and expected to make creative and meaningful engagements over several hours. Better play facilities are to be found in some Burger King and McDonald's fast-food outlets.

Supervised contact

Being supervised and observed under contact conditions is an artificially constructed situation, with no script to follow regarding the kind of behaviour to be expected from each participant, including the supervisor. Much of it has to be guessed. Long sessions with one and often more children under such conditions can prove very demanding, intense and nerve racking – far more so if watched by one and sometimes two supervisors, even though the parent may have no history of violence or threatening behaviour. When at home, it is unusual for a parent to give so much undivided attention to a single child for so long. More likely they will be engaged in other activities in the kitchen, at the back or front patio, or go out to the park or local shops. What parents

can or cannot say during contact can vary between authorities and sometimes between different supervising workers. This only adds to parental anxiety. They may then be criticised for not being spontaneous. Even stricter controls operate when the child is about or has moved to a 'permanent' placement. For example, for the parent to mention their new house or say they redecorated a child's room, or stress that the family were missing them, could be interpreted as wanting the child home and therefore inappropriate.

Once a child is accommodated, contact becomes the main, and often the only, medium for observing parental behaviours. In the absence of other evidence, decisions of whether or not to rehabilitate a child home often rely on parental behaviour during contact. The ambiguity of the role of the supervising worker is highlighted when faced with the dilemma of whether to give the parent feedback. In my experience, those who perceive their role as that of a non-participant observer simply observe, record and later report to a review. But it is of no help telling a mother after a period of time that, owing to her lack of parenting skills, her contact will be drastically reduced. Some supervisors do offer support and advice, making suggestions, undertaking modelling or role play and using video playbacks. Adopting the latter role involves striking a balance between support and constructive criticism; otherwise it can be experienced as undermining confidence. Parents, many of whom already have low self-esteem, are more likely to be receptive to advice and suggestions, and even criticism, if it comes from supervisors with whom they have a positive relationship. With the frequent change of social workers, the lack of time to promote interpersonal relationships and the traditional antipathy felt by many parents towards professionals who have been instrumental in the child's removal, a collaborative atmosphere can prove difficult to establish.

While some parental and child behaviours during contact are clearly positive or negative, uncertainty remains. A usual double-bind is the frequently heard comment that if a child does not appear to be upset on parting from a parent after contact, then contact is unimportant to them. The opposite can also be said – namely that if the child is upset at the end, contact may have to be reduced or even stopped. Yet again, there can be a number of possible explanations for these reactions, many of them unrelated to what takes place during meetings. There needs to be awareness of the wider context of past events in a child's life and the current situation, such as what goes on within the foster or residential setting, yet some of those who supervise contact know little or nothing about this dimension.

All of this makes it difficult to establish a fair curriculum as the rules are riddled with contradictions. Parents are criticised for not being sufficiently proactive but also for being too dominant. Too many limits are interpreted as stifling, while laxity is condemned. Children and parents who have not seen much of each other often look upon parental concessions as a sign of affection and on controls as rejection. Parents, who already feel great insecurity about their parenting and guilty for the children being in care, will see enforcing controls as making them feel 'bad' and rejecting, especially when they will not see the child for some time to make it up. Not surprisingly, children sense and play into such feelings.

Parents have to feel very secure and convinced that what matters to their child is their presence if they are to resist demands for bigger presents and expensive toys, or for sweets, or to forbid jumping on the furniture or playing with the electric switches. However, had they felt that confident about their parenting and secure in themselves, possibly the children would not have entered care in the first place.

So, can this situation be considered a level playing field?

Conclusion

This review of contact illustrates the difficulties of providing substitute care and the danger of unsubstantiated generalisations. The discussion shows that while we have learned a lot in recent years, there is clearly much more to discover before we can be confident about what we do. BAAF's work is clearly cut out.

Finally, I am aware that this is a special edition to mark BAAF's 30th birthday. I have known the journal under different names for a number of decades before it was relaunched in its present format. It is not an exaggeration to say how fortunate we are in Britain to have a journal of this calibre that has struck a nice balance between the publication of researched-based articles and the sharing of practice experience. Long may it continue.

References

Ames Reed J, *We have Learned a Lot from Them: Foster care for young people with learning difficulties*, Barkingside: Barnardo's/National Children's Bureau, 2003

Berridge D and Cleaver H, *Foster Home Breakdown*, Oxford: Blackwell, 1987

Berridge D, *Foster Care: A research review*, London: The Stationery Office, 1997

Bowlby J, *Attachment and Loss, Vol. 1*, London: Hogarth Press, 1969

Butler-Sloss E, reported in *The Times*, 10 November 2001

Cleaver H, 'Contact: the social worker's experience', *Adoption & Fostering* 21:4, pp 34–40, 1997/8

Cleaver H, *Fostering Family Contact*, London: The Stationery Office, 2000

Fratter J, Rowe J, Sapsford D and Thoburn J, *Permanent Family Placement: A decade of experience*, London: BAAF, 1991

Fursland E, *Social Networking and Contact: How social workers can help adoptive families*, London: BAAF, 2010

Hess PM and Proch KO, *Contact: Managing visits to children looked after away from home*, London: BAAF, 1993

Hetherington EM and Stanley-Hagan M, 'The adjustment of children with divorced parents: a risk and resiliency perspective', *Journal of Child Psychology and Psychiatry* 40:1, pp 129–40, 1999

Holman R, 'Exclusive and inclusive concepts of fostering', in Triseliotis J (ed), *New Developments in Adoption and Foster Care*, London: Routledge & Kegan Paul, 1980

Holman R, *Trading in Children*, London: Routledge & Kegan Paul, 1973

Howe D and Steele M, 'Contact in cases in which children have been traumatically abused or neglected by their birth parents', in Neil D and Howe D (eds), *Contact in Adoption and Permanent Foster Care*, London: BAAF, 2004

Katz L, Maluccio L and Cordes K, *Concurrent Planning*, Seattle, WA: Lutheran Social Services, 1994

Loxterkamp L, 'Contact and truth: the unfolding predicament in adoption and fostering', *Clinical Child Psychology and Psychiatry* 14:3, pp 423–35, 2009

McCauley C, *Children in Long Term Fostering*, Aldershot: Avebury, 2002

Millham S, Bullock R, Hosie K and Haak M, *Lost in Care*, London: Gower, 1986

Monck E, Reynolds J and Wigfall V, *The Role of Concurrent Planning*, London: BAAF, 2003

Neil E and Howe D (eds), *Contact in Adoption and Permanent Foster Care*, London: BAAF, 2004

Schaffer HR, *Making Decisions about Children*, Oxford: Basil Blackwell, 1990

Scharff SJ (ed), *The Psychodynamic Image: John D Sutherland on self in society*, London: Routledge, 2007

Sinclair I, *Fostering Now: Messages from research*, London: Jessica Kingsley Publishers, 2005

Sinclair I, Baker C, Wilson K and Gibbs I, *Foster Children: Where they go and how they get on*, London: Jessica Kingsley Publishers, 2005

Smith C and Logan J, *After Adoption: Direct contact and relationships*, London: Routledge & Kegan Paul, 2004

Thoburn J and Rowe J, 'Research: a snapshot of permanent family placement', *Adoption & Fostering* 12:3, pp 29–34, 1988

Trasler G, *In Place of Parents*, London: Routledge & Kegan Paul, 1960

Triseliotis J, 'Maintaining the links in adoption', *British Journal of Social Work* 21:4, pp 401–14, 1991

Triseliotis J, Borland M and Hill M, *Delivering Foster Care*, London: BAAF, 2000

Wedge P and Mantle G, *Sibling Groups and Social Work*, Aldershot: Gower, 1991

Weinstein EA, *The Self-image of the Child*, New York: Russell Sage Foundation, 1960

Wilkinson C, *Prospect, Process and Outcome in Foster Care*, Unpublished M.Phil. thesis, Edinburgh University, 1988

Thirty years of listening to children?

Alison McLeod looks back over the last 30 years to see how the theory, policy and practice of listening to children in the UK have developed.

Alison McLeod is Senior Lecturer in Social Work, University of Cumbria

Key words: listening to children, children's rights, social work, law, child care policy

Thirty-one years ago, the veteran campaigner for children's rights, Mia Kellmer Pringle, wrote:

Children are the largest minority group that has no voice, no vote, very little influence and – with a few exceptions – very few rights in law. (Kellmer Pringle, 1979 p 193)

The following year, 1980, BAAF was formed and by coincidence I commenced my social work training. So, now seems a good time to pose the questions: Have children more of a voice now than they had when Kellmer Pringle wrote those words? What influence, if any, has BAAF had in encouraging agencies and practitioners to listen to the young people they work with?

Does it matter?

The reasons why it is important for children to be heard, though familiar, bear restating. The most obvious is that if we do not listen to them, we cannot protect them from abuse and neglect. Not listening to maltreated children 'entraps them in lethal silence' (Freeman, 1999, p 52). Less obviously, children who are never given opportunities to make decisions for themselves may grow up less able to exercise choice responsibly (Hillman, 2006; Leeson, 2007). Being listened to also enhances children's well-being: it promotes a positive sense of identity (Eide and Winger, 2005), helps them feel more in control (Butler *et al*, 2002), assists in combating stress (Munro, 2001), develops their capacity for problem-solving (Sinclair, 2000) and contributes to their resilience (Gilligan, 1999). Furthermore, consulting with the young people who

use a service can improve its design and delivery (Kinney, 2005; Cairns and Brannen, 2005). There are pragmatic reasons, too, why professionals working with children should consider their views: research from various settings indicates that interventions will be more successful if they are planned in partnership with service users (Triseliotis *et al*, 1995; Veeran, 2004).

Finally, listening to children is a matter of ethics and human rights (Freeman, 1999). It is disrespectful and disempowering to ignore a person of any age and the fact that a service user is under the age of 18 does not make them any less a person. This is a view that has become increasingly accepted in the UK over the last 30 years.

Changing law and policy

Children's rights is a relatively modern concept. UK law was formerly based on a view of children as adjuncts to their parents, rather than individuals in their own right (Kellmer Pringle, 1979). Early attempts to define children's rights concentrated on their welfare and protection (Fuller, 1951). By the 1980s, however, a new approach was developing which saw the primary right as a political one – the right to be heard (Freeman, 1983) – a change that was paralleled by the development of a 'new sociology of childhood' that stressed the individuality and capacity of children as active agents shaping their own worlds (James and Prout, 1990). The law has gradually been reformed to a position where children have incrementally more say in decisions affecting them as they grow towards adulthood, a process described as 'dynamic self-determination' (Thomas, 2002).

The milestone 'Fraser ruling' of 1986 had a significant impact on a young person's right to make his or her own decisions, if of sufficient 'understanding and intelligence' to be capable of making up his or her mind on the matter requiring decision (House of Lords ruling, *Gillick v West Norfolk & Wisbech Health Authority*, 1986). However, 1989 was even more important for children's rights. After a decade of debate, the UN Convention was agreed. The 'lynchpin' of the Convention (Lansdown, 1992) is Article 12, which states:

The child who is capable of forming his or her own views shall be assured the right to express those views freely in all matters affecting the child, the views of the child being given due weight in accordance with his or her age and maturity. (United Nations, 1989)

In the same year, the Children Act 1989 was passed applying to England and Wales (the broadly similar Children Act (Scotland) 1995 followed a few years later). Central to young people's voice under English law is section 1(3)a:

A court shall have regard in particular to the ascertainable wishes and feelings of the child concerned (considered in the light of his age and understanding).

The Act gave young people a number of other rights, including the right to be consulted and involved in plans for their own care and to make a formal complaint about services received under the Act. More legislation promoting children's rights has followed: in England and Wales the Family Law Act 1996, the Adoption and Children 2002, the Children Act 2004, the Child Care Act 2006 and the Children and Young Persons Act 2008, each of which has extended the range of situations in which children have a legal right to be heard.

Voluminous guidance and regulations spelt out how the provisions of the 1989 Act were to be implemented, starting a trend whereby central government dictates how child care law is to be translated into practice. A series of policy documents (Department of Health, 1998; Department for Education and Skills, 2003; Department of Health, 2004; Department for Children, Schools and Families, 2007) all stressed the importance of listening to children at both individual and service level, in all public services. There has been a plethora of official advice on how to do this (Children and Young People's Unit, 2001; Kirby *et al*, 2003; Department for Education and Skills, 2004; HM Government, 2005). Targets and performance indicators were set for children's involvement in planning, and meeting these influenced a local authority's access to funding.

The child's right to be heard is thus firmly established in law and policy, and it would appear that the Government has made efforts to ensure that the law is implemented, using a combination of reward and sanction approaches. That much has changed in the last 30 years. But has the experience of children altered?

A revolution in practice?

Participation, it can be argued, begins at home. The evidence on our families, schools and communities, however, is that children's democratic involvement in them is at best limited, at worst tokenistic (Alderson, 2002; Leach, 2003; Mayall, 2005). The Forum for Rural Children and Young People (2005, p 7) concluded there was 'little concrete evidence that adults have taken steps to ensure young people's real involvement' in planning processes. Evaluating the Children's Fund initiative, Spicer and Evans (2006, p 178) similarly concluded that this had failed to involve children at a strategic level. They suggested that the participation agenda risked only 'serving and legitimating adult/professionally driven agendas'.

The picture for vulnerable children is equally disappointing. Children in special schools in Northern Ireland felt their voices were not heard or their views respected (Lundy and Kilpatrick, 2006). Young people in psychiatric hospital did not feel heard: 'Sure they'll listen. It's a bit different listening from actually doing something!' (Young person quoted in Le François, 2007, p 96). Involvement of young people in health care planning was 'piecemeal and marginal' (Day, 2008, p 7). Children in touch with social care services had little say in decisions made about them (Aubery and Dahl, 2006). In addition, a mass of evidence shows that the more marginalised a young person, the less likely he or she is to be heard (Cairns and Brannen, 2005; Chand, 2005; Franklin and Sloper, 2006).

The evidence on looked after children is no better. Their involvement in care planning and decision-making still appears poor (Leeson, 2007; Archard and Skivenes, 2009). Participation in LAC reviews often falls short of being meaningful (McLeod, 2007), their involvement in care proceedings is strictly limited (Thoburn, 2004) and many still feel that their social workers do not listen to them (Gaskell, 2010) or give them the information and explanations they need (Winter, 2010).

Why should practice still lag behind theory and aspiration? It may not just be that practitioners lack skills in communicating with children. Archard and Skivenes (2009) found that child care social workers appeared to have a range of sensitive and appropriate strategies for opening up a dialogue with a child. However, although they elicited children's views, they then often discounted them, arguing that the child was not competent to make the relevant decision. Winter (2009), for example, found that social workers routinely underestimated the potential of younger children to make their own decisions, blaming this on a theoretical base grounded in an 'ages and stages' view of child development. Day (2008) saw the issue as a question of power, wondering whether health professionals were ambivalent about young people's participation in planning because by empowering patients they disempowered themselves. Kelley (2006) similarly illustrated how political pressures can militate against allowing young people genuine influence on policy. Gaskell (2010) blamed resource issues for social workers' failure to accord with young people's wishes: more appropriate placements were just not available. Many observers

of the current child care scene bewail the volume of paperwork social workers have to wade through and the tendency to delegate skilled direct work to unqualified workers (Ruch, 2005; Romaine *et al*, 2007). It is clear that our collective failures to listen to children have multiple causes that are not easy to unravel.

Taking the long view

Faced with the weight of evidence of indifferent practice, it would be easy to become disheartened. Of course we have a long way to go, but that should not blind us to the distance we have already travelled. The picture can look quite different when put in its historical context.

When I started research into listening to children in the mid-1990s, I could find very little published on the topic; now there is a plethora of research (Holland, 2009) and practice guides (Jones, 2003; McLeod, 2008; Lefevre, 2010). Children also have a growing awareness of their rights and are represented by organisations like the Who Cares? Trust, the Care Leavers' Association and a National Voice. In the late nineties only a quarter of looked after children knew how to make a complaint (Aiers and Kettle, 1998); a decade later the figure was over three-quarters (Morgan, 2009). In addition, there have been significant changes in practice: Sinclair researched statutory reviews in the eighties, and found that young people were present at only two per cent of the meetings; by the late nineties, she found the figure had risen to 55 per cent (Sinclair, 1984, 1998). That represents a very considerable change that should not be belittled, even though it remains a challenge to move from mere attendance to meaningful involvement.

Is it realistic to expect practice to transform itself as fast as expectations have? Balancing children's welfare and self-determination rights is not always easy or straightforward (Thomas, 2002; Schofield, 2005). If we look at each piece of research that highlights poor practice, almost all find an acceptance among professionals that children have a right to be heard and most identify some good work. A service may be flawed (Pithouse and Parry, 2005) yet the very fact that the service exists can represent an advance. Perhaps after all we should do more celebrating of our achievements and agonise less about the slow pace of progress.

The role of BAAF
In BAAF's 30th birthday year, how should we evaluate its contribution to this slow but appreciable progress towards hearing the voices of the young? For me personally it has been signifi-cant. In the mid-1980s I attended a BAAF training course, *In Touch with Children* (Bailey and Batty, 1984).[1] The course advocated a holistic and relationship-based approach to child care social work and focused on developing skills in communication with children and direct work. The trainers employed by BAAF at that time (Donal Giltinan, Maureen Thom and Sally Wassell) were passionate and charis-matic. It was an inspiration to me and sent my career on a new trajectory.

There was no internet in those days and I had no access to an academic library. The only serious social work journal I regularly came across was *Adoption & Fostering* and I learned about current research findings through this and other BAAF publications, due to their enlightened policy of sending multiple free copies of their journal and publications to member agencies. Almost the only books and materials I could find on direct work with children were also BAAF publications (Jewett, 1984; Ryan and Walker, 1985; Aldgate and Simmonds, 1988; King and Chaplin, 1989). There must have been other practitioners who, like me, developed their practice and learned to listen to children through the work of this organisation.

What of BAAF's wider contribution to children's rights? Overall, I believe its contribution to raising standards of child-centred practice in this country has been appreciable. Looking at *Adoption & Fostering* journal since 1980, it cannot be said that the voice of the child has been at the top of BAAF's agenda but it has been a consistent theme and one which in the last decade has become more embedded. Young people are often now represented at its conferences, and their voices feature strongly in many current publications although, as far as I am aware, young people have not been involved at a strategic level in BAAF as an organisation.

Are we listening yet?
The accumulated evidence on listening to children thus indicates that there have been significant changes in law and policy over the last 30 years, so that young people now have substan-tially increased legal rights to self-determination. It would also appear that there has been some shift in public and professional opinion, though this shift may not be as fundamental as one might hope. Research on children's perspec-tives and the availability of guidance on communicating with children have increased markedly, and there are signs of patchy and equivocal but perceptible shifts in practice towards taking children more seriously. Giving weight to child-ren's views continues to challenge professionals, however, and standards of practice in listening to children remain weak overall. As Sinclair commented: 'Every advance in standards simply serves to show how much there is still to achieve.' (Sinclair, 1998, p 8).

With a new government committed to cuts in public spending and with an apparent wish to dismantle much that was set up by its predecessor, even the limited progress achieved in listening to children so far may be under threat, particularly given that children's partici-pation, if it is to be meaningful, requires

---

[1] *Editor's note*: BAAF will be publishing a similar training course, together with a Practice Guide on Communicating with Children, in early 2011.

realistic and sustained resourcing (Spicer and Evans, 2006; McLeod, 2010). Let us hope that this government are themselves willing to listen to the voices of the next generation: 'Everybody should be equal and have a right to say their opinion' (child quoted in Morgan, 2010, p 9). Is that too much to ask?

References

Aiers A and Kettle J, *When Things Go Wrong: Young people's experience of getting access to the complaints procedure in residential care*, London: National Institute for Social Work, 1998

Alderson P, 'Civil rights in schools', *Highlight* 191, London: National Children's Bureau, 2002

Aldgate J and Simmonds J, *Direct Work with Children*, London: BAAF/Batsford, 1988

Archard D and Skivenes M, 'Hearing the child', *Child & Family Social Work* 14: 4, pp 391–9, 2009

Aubery C and Dahl S, 'Children's voices: the views of vulnerable children on their service providers and the relevance of services they receive', *British Journal of Social Work* 36:1, pp 21–9, 2006

Bailey N and Batty D (eds), *In Touch with Children: Training materials*, London: BAAF, 1984

Butler I, Scanlan L, Robinson M, Douglas G and Murch M, 'Children's involvement in their parents' divorce', *Children & Society* 16:2, pp 89–102, 2002

Cairns L and Brannen M, 'Promoting the human rights of children and young people: the "Investing in Children" experience', *Adoption & Fostering* 29:1, pp 78–87, 2005

Chand A, 'Do you speak English? Language barriers in child protection social work with minority ethnic families', *British Journal of Social Work* 35:6, pp 807–21, 2005

Children and Young People's Unit, *Learning to Listen: Core principles for the involvement of children and young people*, London: Department for Education and Skills, 2001

Day C, 'Children and young people's involvement and participation in mental health care', *Child and Adolescent Mental Health* 13:1, pp 2–8, 2008

Department for Children, Schools and Families,

The Children's Plan: Building better futures, London: TSO, 2007

Department for Education and Skills, *Every Child Matters*, London: TSO, 2003

Department for Education and Skills, *Pupil Participation Guidance – Working Together: Giving children and young people a say*, London: TSO, 2004

Department of Health, *The Quality Protects Programme: Transforming children's services*, London: Department of Health, 1998

Department of Health, *National Services Framework for Children, Young People and Maternity Services*, London: TSO, 2004

Eide B and Winger N, 'From the children's point of view: methodological and ethical challenges', in Clark A, Kjørholt A and Moss P (eds), *Beyond Listening: Children's perspectives on early childhood services*, Bristol: Policy Press, 2005

Forum for Rural Children and Young People, *Participation in our Village: Involving children and young people in the development of parish and town plans*, London: National Children's Bureau, 2005

Franklin A and Sloper P, *Participation of Disabled Children and Young People in Decision-making Relating to Social Care*, York: University of York Social Policy Research Unit, 2006

Freeman M, 'The concept of children's rights', in Geach H and Szwed E (eds), *Providing Civil Justice for Children*, London: Edward Arnold, 1983

Freeman M, 'The right to be heard', *Adoption & Fostering* 22:4, pp 50–59, 1999

Fuller E, *The Right of the Child*, London: Gollancz, 1951

Gaskell C, ' "If the social worker had called, at least it would show they cared": Young care leavers' perspectives on the importance of care', *Children & Society* 24:2, pp 136–47, 2010

Gilligan R, 'Enhancing the resilience of children and young people in public care by mentoring their talents and interests', *Child & Family Social Work* 4:3, pp 187–96, 1999

Hillman M, 'Children's rights and adults' wrongs', *Children's Geographies* 4:1, pp 61–7, 2006

HM Government, *The Common Core of Skills and Knowledge for the Children's Work Force*, London: TSO, 2005

Holland S, 'Listening to children in care: a review of methodological and theoretical approaches to understanding looked after children's perspectives', *Children & Society* 23:3, pp 226–35, 2009

James A and Prout A (eds), *Constructing and Reconstructing Childhood*, London: Falmer, 1990

Jewett C, *Helping Children Cope with Separation and Loss*, London: BAAF, 1984

Jones D, *Communicating with Vulnerable Children*, London: Gaskell, 2003

Kelley N, 'Children's involvement in policy formation', *Children's Geographies* 4:1, pp 37–44, 2006

Kellmer Pringle M, 'Children's rights and parental rights and obligations', in Doxiadis S (ed), *The Child in the World of Tomorrow*, Oxford: Pergamon Press, 1979

King P and Chaplin P, *Talking Pictures*, London: BAAF, 1989

Kinney L, 'Small voices, powerful messages', in Clark A, Kjørholt A and Moss P (eds), *Beyond Listening: Children's perspectives on early childhood services*, Bristol: Policy Press, 2005

Kirby P, Lanyon C, Cronin K and Sinclair R, *Building a Culture of Participation: Involving children and young people in policy, service planning, delivery and evaluation – handbook*, London: Department for Education and Skills, 2003

Lansdown G, 'Key right is the child's right to be heard', *Childright* 11, p 4, 1992

Leach R, 'Children's participation in family decision-making', *Highlight* 196, London: National Children's Bureau, 2003

Leeson C, 'My life in care: experiences of non-participation in decision-making processes', *Child & Family Social Work* 12:3, pp 268–77, 2007

Lefevre M, *Communicating with Children and Young People: Making a difference*, Bristol: Policy Press, 2010

Le François B, 'Children's participation rights: voicing opinions in in-patient care', *Child and Adolescent Mental Health* 12:2, pp 94–97, 2007

Lundy L and Kilpatrick R, 'Children's rights and special educational needs: findings from research conducted for the Northern Ireland Commissioner for children and young people', *Support for Learning* 21:2, pp 57–63, 2006

Mayall B 'The social condition of UK child-hoods: children's understandings and their implications', in Mason J and Fattore T (eds), *Children Taken Seriously in Policy and Practice*, London: Jessica Kingsley Publishers, 2005

McLeod A, *Evaluation of 8s to 10s Participation Project: Baseline survey report*, Unpublished paper, 2007

McLeod A, *Listening to Children: A practitioner's guide*, London: Jessica Kingsley Publishers, 2008

McLeod A, ' "A friend and an equal": do young people in care seek the impossible from their social workers?', *British Journal of Social Work* 40:3, pp 772–88, 2010

Morgan R, *Children's Care Monitor 2009*, Manchester: Ofsted, 2009

Morgan R, *Children on Rights and Responsibilities: A report of children's views by the Children's Rights Director for England*, Manchester: Ofsted, 2010

Munro E, 'Empowering looked after children', *Child & Family Social Work* 6:2, pp 129–37, 2001

Pithouse A and Parry O, 'Children's advocacy in Wales: organisational challenges for those who commission and deliver advocacy for looked after children', *Adoption & Fostering* 29:4, pp 45–56, 2005

Romaine M, Turley T and Tuckey N, *Preparing Children for Permanence: A guide to undertaking direct work for social workers, foster carers and adoptive parents*, London: BAAF, 2007

Ruch G, 'Relationship-based practice and reflective practice: holistic approaches to childcare social work', *British Journal of Social Work* 10:2, pp 111–23, 2005

Ryan T and Walker R, *Life Story Work*, London: BAAF, 1985

Schofield G, 'The voice of the child in family placement decision-making: a developmental model', *Adoption & Fostering* 29:1, pp 29–44, 2005

Sinclair R, *Decision-making in Statutory Reviews on Children in Care*, Aldershot: Gower, 1984

Sinclair R, 'Involving children in planning their care', *Child & Family Social Work* 3:1, pp 137–42, 1998

Sinclair R, *Quality Protects Research Briefing No 3: Young people's participation*, London: Department of Health, 2000

Spicer N and Evans R, 'Developing children and young people's participation in strategic processes: the experience of the Children's Fund initiative', *Social Policy and Society* 5:2, pp 177–88, 2006

Thoburn J, 'Involving children in planning and reviewing services', in Lord Justice Thorpe and Cadbury J (eds), *Hearing the Children*, Bristol: Jordan, 2004

Thomas N, *Children, Family and the State: Decision-making and child participation*, Bristol: Policy Press, 2002

Triseliotis J, Borland M, Hill M and Lambert L, *Teenagers and the Social Work Services*, London: HMSO, 1995

United Nations Convention on the Rights of the Child, Geneva: United Nations, 1989

Veeran V, 'Working with street children: a child-centred approach', *Child Care in Practice* 10:4, pp 359–66, 2004

Winter K 'Relationships matter: the problems and prospects for social workers' relationships with young children in care', *Child & Family Social Work* 14:4, pp 450–60, 2009

Winter K, 'The perspectives of young children in care about their circumstances and the implications for social work practice', *Child & Family Social Work* 15:2, pp 186–95, 2010

Access to information Progress and perils

Julia Feast discusses BAAF's role in securing the right of adopted people to have access to information about their origins and how perceptions regarding this right have changed over time

Julia Feast is Policy, Research and Development Consultant, BAAF

Key words: adoption records, origins, access to information, post-care adults, legislation, Data Protection Act 1998, BAAF

Introduction

In the UK the right of adopted people to have access to information about their origins is well established. Each country has legislation that allows adopted people to receive details enabling them to obtain a copy of their original birth certificate and the opportunity to reconnect with birth family members if they so wish. However, we should not become complacent that this hard-fought right will go unchallenged in the future. It is crucial to continue to evidence the wide-ranging benefits that accessing information can have for adopted people and their families. The same applies to people who have been brought up in care or been born as a result of donor-assisted conception, but unfortunately for these groups it is not so easily achieved.

Over the past 30 years, BAAF has played a significant role in promoting the information rights of adopted people and the rights of birth relatives to request intermediary services so that they can let an adoptive relative know that they would like to have contact.

BAAF has led or partnered many campaigns, for instance, during the passage of the Adoption and Children Bill (2001), which proposed to limit drastically adopted people's rights to identifying information. Together with organisations such as The Children's Society and NORCAP, it brought this proposal to the attention of the adoption community and was successful in overturning it.

BAAF has also strived to ensure that the knowledge gained about the importance of accessing information concerning genetic heritage is used to inform and educate other situations

where children are raised in families where there is no genetic link with either one or both of the parents, such as in donor-assisted conception. The organisation was at the forefront in promoting the identity needs of the child (BAAF et al, 1984; Walby and Symons, 1990).

More recently, during the passage of the Children Act 2008, BAAF joined with other organisations to campaign (unfortunately without success) for a new legislative framework to ensure that post-care adults are on the same footing as adopted people in terms of access to information and are not restricted in obtaining comprehensive details about their family background and records relating to their time in care.

In celebration of BAAF's 30th anniversary, this article will therefore explore the importance of accessing information and explain why it is crucial that we do not become complacent in the belief that all bodes well for the future.

Perceptions over time

In the very early days of adoption, people's perception was that it would not only sever the legal ties with the birth family, but the emotional ones as well. In the 1950s, a leaflet produced for adoptive parents on what they should tell their child about adoption advised that:

. . . provided that the child has not grown up with the idea that his adoptive parents do not love him, or that there is some mystery about his origins, he will not dwell unduly on these matters or want to get in touch with his natural parents. (Standing Conference of Societies Registered for Adoption, 1950)

It is nowadays accepted by all those in the adoption community that this is simply not true, and that it is important for children to be given information about their origins and family background and the reasons why they were placed for adoption. Adoption does not end when the order has been made; it is a life-long process, not just for adopted people themselves but for anyone who has been affected by it.

Today, adoptive parents are encouraged and supported to talk to their son or daughter about his or her beginnings (Morrison, 2007; Wolfs, 2008, 2010). All children should have life story books with photos of significant people and places so that they can know their histories, build a stronger sense of identity and appreciate who they are and 'what makes them tick' (Camis, 2001; Shah and Argent, 2006; Cairns and Fursland, 2008).

Communicating about a child's origins and adoption and telling him or her difficult and distressing information are not easy and have to be done in an age-appropriate way. However, adopted people need to have information and facts about their origins and family history; talking and telling is an integral part of the adoption process. Research studies have shown that just because a person does not raise the subject of their adoption and origins and ask questions, it does not mean they do not want to talk about it (Howe and Feast, 2003).

The need for adopted people to have access to information about their origins was recognised when the Children Act 1975 came into force. The legislation made the provision for adopted people in England and Wales to have the right, once they reached the age of 18 years, to apply for the necessary information and to obtain a copy of their original birth certificate. This had always been a right for people in Scotland, as its 1930 Act addressed this at the time. In Northern Ireland it became a right in 1987.

The opening up of adoption records was a significant step and made a clear statement about adopted people's rights to have an opportunity to know more about their original background. The legislation was retrospective. Some may say that this was a brave step to take at that time, as societal attitudes were very different from today, when it is generally accepted that access to information and/or making contact with birth family members can be a positive experience

This was further reflected in the guidance notes that were issued by the Department of Health and Social Security (DHSS) for counsellors undertaking Access to Birth Records in England and Wales when the legislation came into force in 1976. These recognised the importance of adopted people accessing information about their origins and made it clear that the 'counsellor' does not have the right to withhold basic information. However, there was great concern about the impact on birth parents and other relatives should the adopted person decide that they wanted to trace and contact them. The emphasis was very much on 'leave well alone', as portrayed in the following quotation:

The possible distress and disappointment at not being able to trace one's parents or of being rebuffed should be mentioned. The counsellor may advise against continuing the search because of the other people who could be hurt. The applicant must be helped to accept responsibility for the pain he might cause to himself and to others if he pursues his quest . . . (DHSS, 1976, p 6)

But as with opening up records, the fears expressed at this time have not been realised. Instead, empirical studies support the legislative change that occurred in 1975, showing that having the opportunity and choice to seek background information and make contact with birth relatives can bring a range of psychological benefits to many adopted people and their birth parents without affecting the relationships in the family (Howe and Feast, 2003; Triseliotis et al, 2005).

BAAF was at the forefront of producing advice notes for all those affected by these changes, including a practical guide to assist practitioners to provide high-quality birth record counselling, access to information and intermediary support services (Hodgkins, 1991).

Access to information denied: a changing climate?

The opportunity to access information and the climate of openness now seem to be under threat. During the past few years some indicators have suggested a move towards restricting adopted people's established right to access information. Regulations 14, 15 and 16 of the Adoption Agencies Regulations 1983 were retained when the Adoption and Children Act 2002 for England and Wales was implemented in December 2005. Regulation 15 provides adoption agencies with the discretion over the information they disclose from their case records in pre-commencement adoptions (ie adoption orders granted before the 30 December 2005). The retention of this regulation is particularly significant for adopted people as it recognises the importance of their ability to access both identifying and non-identifying information about origins and background, but also provides the adoption agency with the discretion to disclose the information.

In May 2008, the Department for Children, School and Families published Practice Guidance on access to information and intermediary services. It was drafted by practitioners who understood the importance of retaining Regulation 15, but unfortunately, the final version has been peppered inappropriately with references to the Data Protection Act 1998. This could have a detrimental affect on current practice and prevent adopted people from accessing information that would help them understand their situation and manage their lives.

When working with people adopted from overseas, the Guidance also advises that sensitive information about a subject, such as the birth mother, must not be disclosed to the adopted person without the subject's permission. Sensitive information includes health or 'racial' or ethnic origin. It is difficult to understand why the Government deemed it necessary to seek a birth mother's permission for such information to be disclosed when 'racial' and ethnic origin is so fundamental to the adopted person's identity.

In the Welsh 2005 Statutory Guidance for Pre-Commencement Adoption Information and Intermediary Services, the word 'non-identifying' within 15.2 Adoption Agency Regulations 1983 has been added. As a result, adopted people in Wales no longer have the same opportunities as their English counterparts to access comprehensive information, as it denies them access to identifying information outside the public domain without the subject's permission.

Such examples show that the climate is changing and taking a backward step. The implications for practice and for adopted people are far reaching, as it means that adopted people could be denied basic and factual information. BAAF has been at the forefront of seeking best practice and policy and clearly continues to have an important role to ensure that adopted people's information needs are not compromised in the future.

The Data Protection Act 1998 and post-care adults

The Data Protection Act 1998 aimed to enhance people's access to information rather than restrict it. However, some local authorities and voluntary agencies are afraid of 'getting it wrong' about what information can be shared, particularly in relation to access to third-party information (Goddard *et al*, 2005). Some organisations prefer to play safe and restrict information rather than exercise their legal discretion to disclose it.

Post-care adults who want to obtain access to information on file now have to make an application under the legislative framework provided by the Data Protection Act 1998. Unfortunately, a significant number of them experience great difficulty obtaining basic information about their family background, as there is a general assumption that the law does not entitle the post-care adult to acquire third-party information without the permission of that third party (see Care Leavers Association website). For example, an agency may be willing to tell the post-care adult that they came into care because their mother had to go into hospital, but decide not to divulge the reason, believing this to be 'third-party' information which infringes on the mother's privacy. Or an organisation may decide not to tell the post-care adult the names and ages of any brothers and sisters they have without those siblings' permission. Yet in an ordinary family, this information would always be known and shared.

It is not uncommon to hear that the information that the post-care adult eventually receives has swathes of tipexed-out information, so that their family story and time in care make little sense. BAAF has recently published a Good Practice Guide for access to record officers and social workers to help them work with the restrictions of the Data Protection Act and the anomalies it creates for people who have spent all or part of their childhood in care (Feast, 2009a).

Access to information: impact and consequences

Not having access to information can have profound consequences, as illustrated in the case of a woman, aged 52, who discovered that she was adopted. Her brother had died of a genetically inherited condition, so when she married she made an 'informed decision', based on the facts she had, not to have children. She was devastated when she discovered that she had made this decision on the basis of false information.

In the 1980s, there was a huge public outcry and a subsequent government enquiry when it came to light that thousands of children had previously been sent overseas to various countries under child migrant schemes. Many of these children had been told that their parents had died or no longer wanted them when this was actually untrue. As adults, these child migrants described heart-rending accounts of the huge loss they experienced from having all links with their families severed, as well as horrendous experiences of abuse (Humphries, 1996; Parker, 2008).

Making decisions about what inform-

ation can and should be shared is a complex area and one that social workers, adoption workers and access to record officers grapple with on a daily basis. 'Whose information is it?' is an important question that ought to be at the forefront of the decision-making process. There needs to be a thorough consideration of the impact of the decision to disclose information or not, along with the consequences this may have. It is crucial that professionals are accountable for their decision-making process about disclosure of information and that this is clearly recorded in the organisation's file, so reflecting a duty of care.

Lessons learned and using the knowledge

Working in the adoption and fostering arena we are in a privileged position to obtain a greater understanding and knowledge about the importance of knowing one's genetic and social make-up, knowing who you are and where you come from. Given the increasing importance of genetics, every child should have the opportunity to discover their genetic heritage so that they can make informed decisions about their health and well-being. As the science of genetics develops, we are only just beginning to understand the importance of genes and how our inheritance may affect our future well-being.

A great deal has been learned about identity and parenting – that children can grow up forming strong and enduring attachments to adoptive parents while also knowing of their genetic/birth family origins. It is therefore important that the knowledge gained is not just used to make lives better for adopted people, those in care and their families but also for other children, such as those born as a result of donor-assisted conception.

Since the 1950s, when donor conception became an option to solve a person's need for a child, thousands of babies have been born this way. Although the anonymity of egg and sperm donors was lifted in 2004, the majority of children are still unaware that they do not have a genetic link with one or both of their parents, as their parents do not need to tell them. Unlike adoption, there are no official documents that will come into the child's possession to show this (Feast, 2009a).

Parents of donor-conceived children do not have to have any preparation or counselling prior to treatment. So, unlike adoptive and foster carers, many such parents may not have had the opportunity to consider the specific issues that need to be addressed when bringing up a child who is not related to either one or both of them.

Over the past 30 years, BAAF has worked to share the knowledge, experience and expertise it has gained from adoption and fostering and the importance of being truthful about a child's origins, as portrayed in the following quotation:

It is for these reasons we have to ask ourselves some serious questions about AID and other forms of artificial reproduction, for they do not emphasise truthfulness and trust; usually the practice is far from open. It is shrouded in secrecy and deceit. The child is deceived, kinsfolk are deceived, members of the community are deceived. As long as deception is integral to artificial reproduction it may be argued the practice strikes a blow at something fundamental in our society. (BAAF et al, 1984, p 71)

Sadly, this could be a quotation from today, as the welfare and identity needs of the donor-conceived child continue to be overlooked in the medical world of infertility. In fostering and adoption, the child's welfare and the right to know their genetic heritage are of paramount importance; it is therefore worrying that this is viewed so differently in the world of infertility.

Parents of donor-conceived children should learn from adoption and not be fearful that the truth will damage the relationship with their child. It is better for children to know from the beginning and to grow up aware of their donor-conceived status. This would avoid the trauma and damage that comes from being told late and living with the burden of deceit.

Every child's identity is unique and precious and this should be respected. All children should be able to access correct documentation about their genetic parentage. BAAF has not given up on this area and continues to campaign for the information needs and rights of donor-conceived children.

Looking to the future

The value of accessing information should not be underestimated. It is crucial that frontline social workers have the resources and skills to undertake a full family history and obtain other information that will be important for the child should they then end up in care or become adopted. At the stage that decisions are being made about the future placement of a child, gathering accurate and comprehensive information about her or his life is essential.

The Adoption and Children Act 2002 sets out what information should be collected for children who have been adopted on or after 30 December 2005. The Child's Permanence Report (CPR) is of particular significance and should be a document that provides a comprehensive account of his/her background and reasons for the adoption. Where information is not on the CPR but held on file, adoption workers need to obtain views about disclosing it so that the information can be shared.

Information is key to helping people understand who they are and where they come from, and when this is missing or withheld it can have profound consequences for identity formation and the resolution of complex issues from the past.

Making decisions about what information can be shared is never easy but it is important that such decisions are not hampered and shrouded by a culture of fear. Practitioners and managers need to embrace the fact that providing people with accurate and comprehensive information about their origins and family background can offer many benefits. It is crucial, therefore, that we do not become complacent but ensure that future legislation, regulation and policy meet the information needs of adopted people, post-care adults and donor-conceived people to help prevent prejudice, discrimination and injustice.

References

BAAF, BASW and a Scottish Working Party, *Aid and After*, London: BAAF: 1984

Cairns K and Fursland E, *Building Identity: A training programme*, London: BAAF/Akamas Training, 2008

Camis J, *My life and Me*, London: BAAF, 2001

Care Leavers' Association website: www. careleavers.com

Department for Children, Schools and Families (DCSF), *Access to Information and Intermediary Services – Practice Guidance*, London: DCSF, 2008

DHSS, *Access to Birth Records: Notes for counsellors*, London: Department of Health and Social Security, 1976

Feast J, *Access to Information for Post-care Adults: A guide for social workers and access to records officers*, London: BAAF, 2009a

Feast J, 'Birth registration – a time of change', *ChildRight* 257, pp 21–25, 2009b

Goddard J, Feast J and Kirton D, *A Childhood on Paper: Accessing the childcare files of former looked after children in the UK*, Bradford: University of Bradford, 2005

Hodgkins P, *Birth Record Counselling: A practical guide*, London: BAAF, 1991

Howe D and Feast J, *Adoption, Search and Reunion: The long-term experience of adopted adults*, first published by The Children's Society (2000), London: BAAF, 2003

Humphries M, *Empty Cradles*, London: Corgi, 1996

Morrison M, *Talking about Adoption to your child*, London: BAAF, 2007

Parker R, *Uprooted: The shipment of poor children to Canada 1867–1917*, Bristol: Policy Press, 2008

Shah S and Argent H, *Life Story Work: What it is and what it means*, London: BAAF, 2006

Standing Conference of Societies Registered for Adoption, *What shall we Tell our Adopted Child?*, London: Standing Conference of Societies Registered for Adoption, 1950

Triseliotis J, Feast J and Kyle F, *The Adoption Triangle Revisited: A study of adoption search and reunion experiences*, London: BAAF, 2005

Walby C and Symons B, *Who am I? Identity, adoption and human fertilisation*, London: BAAF, 1990

Wolfs R, *Adoption Conversations: What, when and how to tell*, London: BAAF, 2008

Wolfs R, *More Adoption Conversations: What, when and how to tell*, London: BAAF, 2010

Adoption Future legal issues

In a climate of increasing financial constraints, **Judith Masson** identifies some of the challenges still surrounding adoption since the implementation of the Adoption and Children Act 2002, in particular the need to simplify current adoption systems in order that children for whom adoption is the plan can be placed in a permanent family without delay.

Judith Masson is Professor of Socio-legal Studies, University of Bristol

Key words: adoption, adoption law

Introduction

There is a challenging legal climate for those working in adoption. Although it might have been expected that, five years after implementation of the Adoption and Children Act 2002, resolution to the conflicts over when and how to secure permanency through adoption would have been achieved, this appears not to be the case. Concern among the judiciary about making 'draconian decisions' in care cases, lack of trust in local authority social workers and an increasing emphasis on genetic inheritance are resulting in continued questioning of the use of adoption, particularly for children in local authority care where this is against the wishes of birth parents. These challenges are not going to be resolved by major new legislation and must be faced in a climate of reduced resources.

Adoption is generally (and rightly) recognised as a measure of last resort. Its main function is to provide family life with legal parents for children whose birth parents and wider family are un-able or unwilling to provide good enough care. Continued support for the institution of adoption requires public confidence in decision-making, in part-icular that children have the opportunity to remain within their birth family wherever there are suitable kin carers. Within this context, different legal arrangements with different powers and different rights to support for carers provide the opportunity not only to tailor arrangements to children's needs but also to tackle the potential for unfairness which undermines children's welfare.

There is a continual need to make the case for adoption through evidence demonstrating its benefits for children among all concerned with legal proceed-ings – judges, lawyers, children's guard-ians and social workers – and with the general public. Increased understanding about child development, especially the development of the infant brain, under-lines the importance of responsive care for children from birth (Howe, 2005); hence, maximising the benefits of adop-tion necessitates reducing the time taken to achieve placements. But a key conse-quence of the way care proceedings are dealt with in the courts, particularly the concern to avoid adoption, produces the opposite effect, namely to increase the time taken to achieve permanence for children who cannot safely be cared for in their birth families.

The adoption process also creates challenges. While this now ensures that the court approves a decision to plan adoption before children are placed with adoptive carers, the length of time between removal from parents or the beginning of care proceedings and being placed for adoption is very substantial. Children who are adopted are children who have waited, often in a series of temporary placements, and whose early development is likely to have been blighted by drug or alcohol pre-birth, poor parental care and insecurity (Ward *et al*, 2006; Masson *et al*, 2008). It is crucial that decisions are taken, and acted on, without delay. However, the complexity of court and agency pro-cesses and their inter-dependency make it extremely difficult to arrange adoption from care within timescales appropriate for children's optimal development.

The key challenge for those develop-ing adoption law and practice is to ensure that children for whom adoption is the plan are adopted without delay. Work to achieve this must increase professional and public understanding of the benefits of early adoption. Confidence in the adoption system also needs to be raised by ensuring that appropriate assessments of parents and relative carers are completed before adoption plans are made. However, financial constraints on local authorities, legal advice services and the courts mean that decisions can no longer be made as they have been, through long proceedings with repeated, expensive expert assessments.

The human rights context

The European Court of Human Rights has repeatedly reminded states that the aim of public care should be reunification of parent and child (*K and T v Finland; Olsson v Sweden*). This does not mean that there should always be reunification, that adoptions cannot take place without parental consent (*Scott v UK*) or that procedures for decision-making cannot be subject to short time constraints (*Kearns v France*). The court has also regularly noted that parents do not have the right to decisions that undermine their child's welfare (*Johansen v Norway*). What the European Convention requires are decisions made according to the state's laws and procedures, a fair balance between the competing interests of individuals and the community, a proportionate response by the state, and the involvement of those with right to respect for their family life in decisions about families (*Keegan v Ireland*). In applying the Convention, it is crucial to recognise that children have rights to protection (*Z v UK*) and these may necessarily override the rights of parents.

Problems with care proceedings

There have been concerns about the length of time care proceedings take since shortly after the Children Act 1989 was implemented. The average time taken is now more than twice what it was in the early years. This is often considered, especially by lawyers and judges, as a problem caused by insufficient resources but should rather be seen as arising from excessive demands from

the courts that result in huge volumes of paperwork, repeated assessments producing no new information and numerous hearings, which avoid decisions rather then resolve them. Despite attempts by the judiciary to reduce delays in care proceedings, most recently through the Public Law Outline (PLO), their length continues to expand as does their cost. The ever-increasing time taken to obtain decisions from the courts denies many children the opportunity for a permanent placement when they could most benefit, in the first year of their lives.

The simple truth is that if care proceedings are going to be made quicker and cost less, they also have to be made smaller. This means making decisions using the evidence that is available at the start of proceedings rather than seeking to assess parental capacity afresh within the proceedings. It means recognising that past behaviour is able to provide at least as reliable indicator of future conduct as an assessment for the proceedings, undertaken necessarily through a small number of meetings. Of course, it is easy to assert that courts need to obtain expert assessments because of the poor quality of core assessments produced by the local authority. However, the excessive demands on local authorities in terms of assessments, court attendance, arranging and supervising contact, as well as procedures imposed on them, mean that they cannot focus their resources on the key tasks. Moreover, there is very little point in local authorities working to raise the quality and depth of assessments undertaken before application if courts are going to require further assessments, partly at local authority expense, once proceedings have started.

The majority of care cases concern neglect, generally over a substantial period of time, perhaps to previous children. In these cases, much of the expert evidence obtained in care proceedings is used not to help the court make a decision but to prevent it having to do so. Assessments are used to test parental commitment and to encourage parents to accept their limitations. Making cases smaller would mean doing without these assessments and returning the responsibility for making decisions to judges and magistrates. The accepted 'wisdom' that it is better to progress matters by agreement ignores two important considerations: first, the need for decisions in the child's timescale; and second, that the context of care proceedings means that there can be no real consent.

Making care proceedings small also means removing much of care planning from the court arena. The adversarial system is not suitable for planning children's future care; children's services and families need to work together rather than in opposition. The combination of family group conferences and professional panels should operate to generate a plan, with priority given to placement in the family, as the Children and Young Persons Act 2008 requires. Where the family is unable to provide permanent, good enough care, professionals have to step in; planning the child's future would be the responsibility of a small team of professionals, including the child's social worker, operating to a clear timetable and resourced to meet it. The court's role should be limited to ensuring set procedures have been followed and making the necessary orders.

Family placements

The current arrangements for family placement raise the possibility of four different orders (residence, special guardianship, adoption or care) with different legal consequences. However, the majority of kinship carers, including many where local authorities have raised concerns, care for children without any court order. Rather than try to fit kinship carers into specific legal categories in potentially contentious proceedings, there needs to be a focus on children's key needs: permanence and support. Kinship carers should have access to financial support through the benefits/ tax credit system, which recognises their importance to the state and their long-

term commitment to the children, and reflect the real costs of bringing up children. They should also have access to services to help them with the challenges of kinship care, such as supporting children to come to terms with their past experiences. Arrangements agreed within families or through family group conferences should be confirmed through binding family agreements that give relative carers parental responsibility. Family carers have the same responsibilities as parents to do the best for the children they care for. The courts should not have a role in determining contact but families would have access to a mediation and support service to help them reach and maintain agreements. This approach recognises the realities of family life, particularly the different forms of accountability which operate over the life course, and the very real limitations of the family justice system in monitoring and managing relationships.

Adoption

The volume of regulations imposed on adoption agencies is excessive and counter productive, generating points on which local authorities can be challenged rather than securing high standards. It is quite extraordinary that as adoption has become an increasingly professional and specialist service, those making decisions have been subject to so much more guidance. This fails to recognise that professional skill and judgement are an essential part of social work. Drafting, disseminating, implementing and operating guidance require resources, which are taken from service delivery. Procedures should be simple and clear so that those operating them do not require further guidance. Professional practice should be supported by the dissemination of research evidence and good practice derived from it, not by endless regulations and guidance.

The current systems for adoption are far too complex, with the overlapping and competing responsibilities of courts and local authorities. This is a particular problem because the excessive duration of care proceedings has meant that agency and court processes have to be carried out in parallel, so that the court can make a placement order at the end of care proceedings without further delay. Even where placement orders are made at the final hearing in care proceedings, the children concerned are likely to have waited more than a year for this decision. Adoption needs to be simplified too – either through restricting the role of the court or the role of the adoption panel.

Under the current care proceedings process the court considers all the evidence about the child's needs and is in a strong position to decide that adoption is the best solution. Consequently, it can be argued that the role of the panel should be limited to approving adopters and matching, leaving the decision about the principle of adoption to the courts. There are two potential problems with this approach. First, judges have very different views about adoption; it is likely that children who could not be cared for in their families would have widely different opportunities of adoption, depending on which court considered the care proceedings. Second, adoption agencies might have to arrange adoptions where social workers thought adoption was not a suitable plan. This would increase the problems caused by a shortage of adoption placements.

Alternatively, changing care proceedings would allow the court's role to be restricted to establishing significant harm and that the care planning procedures had been followed. The local authority would seek a placement order acting on the recommendation of the panel and the court would have to accept the panel's view of the child's welfare.

Different professionals will have different views about the suggestions for simplifying adoption processes. What each needs to explain is why it is necessary to have both panel systems and court-based care planning.

References

Howe D, *Child Abuse and Neglect*, Basingstoke: Palgrave Macmillan, 2005

Masson J, Pearce J, Bader K, Joyner O, Marsden J and Westlake D, *Care Profiling Study MoJ Research Series 04/08*, London: Ministry of Justice, 2008

Ward H, Munro E and Dearden C, *Babies and Young Children in Care*, London: Jessica Kingsley Publishers, 2006

Case list

Johansen v Norway [1997] 23 EHRR 33 ECtHR

K and T v Finland [2000] 2 FLR 39; [2001] 2 FLR 707 ECtHR

Kearns v France [2008] 1 FLR 888 ECtHR

Keegan v Ireland [1994] 3 FCR 165 ECtHR

Olsson v Sweden [1994] 17 EHRR 134 ECtHR

Scott v UK [2000] 1 FLR 958 ECtHR

Z v UK [2001] 2 FLR 612 ECtHR

Thirty years on The achievements of a voluntary membership organisation*

Tony Hall, **Felicity Collier**, **David Holmes** and **John Simmonds**, all of whom have been closely involved with BAAF since its foundation in 1980, review the organisation's achievements and frustrations with regard to improving the welfare of separated children.

Tony Hall was Director of BAAF (formerly ABAFA), 1978–1986

Felicity Collier was Director, then Chief Executive of BAAF, 1995–2006

David Holmes has been Chief Executive of BAAF since 2006

John Simmonds is BAAF's Director of Policy, Research and Development

Key words: BAAF, adoption and fostering, voluntary membership organisation, history, children's services

Introduction

'People start writing histories when they run out of ideas' retorted the historian Royston Lambert when invited to write something for his school centenary celebrations. But while this article relies in some part on the reminiscences of BAAF officials, it is not a history in the strict sense of the term. 'You can only understand what you are like by explanations from your past' continued Lambert when justifying his subject to a group of sceptical children, so it is in this spirit that four people closely concerned with the organisation came together to consider BAAF's development and future role.

BAAF was officially established in 1980 but this was not a new birth. It emerged from the Association of British Adoption and Fostering Agencies (ABAFA), which had itself expanded from the Association of British Adoption Agencies by the addition of the F word. All of this was largely the brainchild of Jane Rowe, the Director at the time. Jane was an exceptionally gifted and insightful reformer who had a clear view of what a children's service should look like. Assisted by Lydia Lambert, she had conducted and published a large (2,812 children in 33 agencies) and extremely influential piece of research on children in long-term care titled *Children who Wait* (Rowe and Lambert, 1973). As Roy Parker explains in the opening article in this journal, the situation with regard to looked after children was quite different from the situation now; residential care was a frequently used placement and the idea of long-term planning for children was little developed. Nevertheless, the findings from Jane and Lydia's study came as something of a shock: of the 626 children who had been in care for more than six months, were aged under 11 and were not living at home, 22 per cent were in need of a permanent family and were, basically, 'drifting' in the system. These findings coincided with similar research from the US and the growth of a movement seeking 'permanence' for children long separated from their birth families.

Given her startling evidence and an auspicious political climate, Jane, as Director of ABAA, saw the need for the organisation to include fostering. This was because so many of the children who concerned her were in either long-term foster homes or in temporary placements awaiting adoptive families, and adoption was often a way of finding them a family. So, in 1976 ABAA became ABAFA. Naturally, some fostering agencies, such as the National Foster Care Association (NFCA), were worried about this change but Jane argued that so much work was needed to improve substitute care that this should be seen as less of a 'takeover' and more as a robust response to the needs of children at risk of 'drift'. In fact, a merger with NFCA was considered a number of times over the next few years but the membership and aims of the two organisations were not quite compatible, and closer collaboration on a number of projects was seen as a better alternative.

In the late 1970s, there was further pressure to strengthen the organisation. The Children Act 1975, which gave

---

* This article is based on discussions with Roger Bullock, Commissioning Editor, and Miranda Davies, Production Editor, of *Adoption & Fostering*.

more protection to separated children, was running into implementation difficulties and social services departments were only beginning to settle down after the Seebohm (1968) reorganisation of 1971. In 1978, Jane Rowe decided to stand down as Director of ABAFA to concentrate on her research interests. Her successor, Tony Hall, a lecturer in social policy at Bristol University, had acted as a research adviser to Jane on the *Children who Wait* study while a research student at the London School of Economics. Despite this early collaboration and his first book on reception and intake into children's departments (1975), Tony was surprised to be invited to apply for the post. He was not a social worker and claimed to have limited knowledge of child care. His research interests and publications were more generally concerned with social services management and processes.

Tony Hall took up his appointment in September 1978 and before Christmas had reached an agreement with John Fitzgerald, Director of the Adoption Resource Exchange (ARE), about the shape of a merger between the two organisations. 'To an outsider it seemed so obviously necessary,' he said. Both organisations worked in the same field, had the same agency membership, had more than 50 per cent overlap in membership of their governing bodies and were potentially in competition for the same funds. Each organisation's plans for the future projected increasing areas of overlap, provoking either unhelpful competition or the need for constant collaboration. Merger was by far the most sensible option. Once the two management boards were agreed to the principle, the biggest headache seemed to be finding a suitable name. Many supported the existing ABAFA title but this was rejected as seeming too much like a takeover rather than a merger. The rather unsatisfactory name of British Agencies for Adoption and Fostering was the compromise and it took many years (and much media confusion in the interim) before the word 'Agencies' was sensibly replaced with 'Association'.

A new organisation also needed a wider group of trustees and a further link with Bristol University was made when Professor Roy Parker was invited to be Chair in 1980. He was eminently suitable for this post because of his academic standing, his publications on children in care and experience at running a large university department with a distinguished track record of research into services for children and families. His book, *Caring for Separated Children* (1980), discussed in the first article, was obviously extremely pertinent. As well as other aims, Roy wanted BAAF to be a 'streetwise pressure group'. He held the post for six years, the maximum period allowed in the new Articles of Administration, standing down in 1986, the same year that Tony Hall left to become Director of the Central Council for Education and Training in Social Work (CCETSW).

Issues in the early years
In those early years, the dominant issue was improving the situation for 'children who wait'. There were still large numbers of children in long-term care, many in residential provision, who had no prospect of a permanent family, whether with relatives or new carers. An early mission statement from BAAF set the pattern for the future by emphasising that its aim was to provide a service for children in need of families, and not to be a child-finding service for would-be adopters.

There were several more specific concerns within this general aim. The Children Act 1975, in which ABAFA had been heavily involved, had been passed, but much of it remained unimplemented following government agreement with local authorities not to add to their existing workload without additional resources. Nevertheless, directly as a result of ABAFA representations, further key sections of the Act were implemented, including section 26, which, for the first time, allowed adopted people access to their original birth records at the age of 18.

At the same time, the Government

funded a major programme of Children Act-related research. ABAFA managed four projects, all of which were completed on time and published. Research covered permanency (Adcock and White, 1979), long-term foster care (Rowe *et al*, 1984), step-parent adoptions (Masson *et al*, 1983) and transracial adoption (Gill and Jackson, 1983).

The concept of permanency and the relevance of models developed in the US were also debated at BAAF conferences where keynote speakers included the hugely influential Kay Donley and Vera Fahlberg, who affected the attitudes and approaches of a whole generation of child care workers. One initiative emerging from this US experience concerned advertising children requiring placements. Initially, *Be My Parent* was launched as a loose-leaf A4 book, advertised widely and located in the waiting rooms of adoption and fostering agencies, libraries and other public offices. Each page contained the photograph and details of one child or sibling group looking for a new permanent family. This gave rise to regular (free) newspaper adverts – initially in *The Guardian* newspaper – that presented individual children looking for a new home, and a television series with the same purpose. *Be My Parent* later evolved in various stages to the publication that has become so well known today. Those who initially criticised the public advertising of children in this way were rapidly silenced by pointing out the unattractive alternatives for those children and the obvious care with which the newspaper was produced.

These developments highlighted five major issues at the time, which had to be addressed. The first concerned the interpretation of permanence and a view held by some critics, such as the Family Rights Group, the Children's Legal Centre and influential thinkers like Bob Holman, that BAAF's working definition meant, in practice, tearing children away from their birth families and placing them for adoption. After all, they argued, nothing is permanent in life; 'constancy', 'stability' or 'reliability' were better concepts. It was at times

difficult to convince those concerned that permanence meant a child's need for a stable and continuing home, whether with the birth family (preferably), with relatives or with strangers. What was crucial was that whatever the plan, a decision should be made about how best to achieve permanence with a clear sequence of steps to make that happen within the child's timescale. Although BAAF's expertise was with separated children, its approach did not ignore or diminish the importance of family support and reunification services whenever these were possible.

The second issue concerned international adoption. As the supply of healthy white babies available for adoption significantly reduced from the late 1960s onwards, the response of adoption agencies across much of the United States and the rest of Europe was to look to overseas countries for a new source of supply to meet the needs of prospective adopters. This usually meant seeking babies from poorer countries and those affected by war and other devastations. ABAFA, and initially BAAF, were publicly very critical of this practice and sought both to plug loopholes in the UK's border practices and publicise an alternative approach. This was not a popular stance in the media, but it was an excellent platform from which to expose the needs of previously hard-to-place children drifting in local authority care. Largely as a result of this early position, intercountry adoption remains far less prevalent in the UK than in most developed countries around the world.

The third issue, linked with the second, concerned foster care, adoption and 'race'. When applying for funds in 1978 to undertake further research on transracial placements, Tony Hall was able to write that 'there had never been a reaction against the practice in this country of the kind that had occurred in the United States'. Three years later, when the first results from this research were being presented prior to publication, things had changed beyond recognition. The severity of the critical response from black social workers to the practice took everyone by surprise, coinciding as it did with the creation of the Association of Black Social Workers. BAAF's response was to create the Black Perspectives Committee (alongside the existing Medical and Legal Groups) to advise and assist BAAF in the development and presentation of its policies in this area.

BAAF's considered view was that while same-race placements are desirable whenever possible, and more should be done to find black families for black children, children should not be denied families because same-race carers were not available when needed. The nuances of this position were not always reflected in press coverage or by some workers who presented the argument as black children should only be adopted by parents of the same ethnic origin. There was a backlash, too, from white parents (some of whom were 'celebrities') who had adopted black children in the 1960s as a radical gesture to promote a 'melting pot society'. The arguments became extremely heated and policy confusion added to the number of children left to wait. A 1984 BAAF seminar based on the recent publication of Triseliotis and Russell's *Hard to Place: The outcome of adoption and residential care* (1984), added fuel to this storm as it confirmed that rigid views about who were and were not appropriate adopters for black and mixed ethnicity children were reducing the opportunities of many children in need of families, since adoption placements for these children were difficult to find.

A fourth related issue was the definition of the children who were considered fosterable or adoptable. For many years after the implementation of the Children Act 1948, the choice for children entering care was simple: either a foster home or a residential placement. Although in 1964, there were considerable differences in the policies of different authorities – for example, East Suffolk fostered nearly 80 per cent of its children in care, compared with around 30 per cent in Worcester – the criteria for deciding were summarised by the mnemonic

SEMAPHORE, a term used by one deputy children's officer to indicate which new entrants to care should go to the local children's home – siblings, mentally and physically handicapped, older children, recidivists (delinquents) and those already ejected from foster care. These criteria may still have a predictive ring to them but Jane Rowe and other reformers, such as Nancy Hazel (Hazel, 1981) in Kent, worked tirelessly to establish an alternative and positive perspective, leading Jane Rowe to summarise her life's work, in response to a question at a conference in 1990, as 'fostering the unfosterable'.

BAAF's work throughout these early years – through the Resource Exchange and *Be My Parent*, through its publicity machine, through its response to inter-country adoption and its publications – helped to promote the view that no child or sibling group in care is impossible to place in an adoptive home or long-term family placement. By the end of the 1970s, the Exchange had a waiting list for children deemed 'hard to place', including babies of mixed race, Down's syndrome babies and 'handicapped' children, older children and large sibling groups. Placements for these children were considered routine (if not straightforward). Organisations such as Parents for Children developed placement practice that enabled children who were previously thought to be impossible to place to find a secure home.

Finally, as we have seen, the type and ages of children in need of permanent families were changing and many were older and had close links with relatives. The notion of 'open adoption' became possible with arrangements for continuing contact with relatives, especially siblings placed elsewhere. This again brought BAAF into discussion with strong pressure groups, such as those representing the interests of grandparents. In barely a decade, adoption had moved from secrecy (where often adopted children were not told of their status despite agency advice to the contrary) to open adoption and a right of adopted people to have access to their original birth records. Inevitably, BAAF was, in these years, drawn into parallel debates in the field of surrogacy and artificial insemination (AID) and helped to influence the policies and safeguards on these issues.

But not everything was a success. One strange omission was the failure of BAAF to give evidence to the subsequently influential House of Commons Social Services Committee on Children in Care chaired by Renée Short, which reported in 1984. It brought child abuse and neglect more squarely into the discussions about substitute care and so highlighted the psychological and medical dimensions of child placement to which BAAF had to react.

The role of specialist charities in the early years was somewhat different to that which developed later. Government departments initially tended to look to particular voluntary organisations for expertise and funded action in areas of policy and practice of concern to them. Jane Rowe, for example, had been crucial to the framing of the 1975 Act and ABAFA/BAAF was seen as offering a link between policy, research and practice at implementation. This spirit of collaboration declined in the 1980s when much activity was drawn back into government and quangos, which were easier for the Government to control. BAAF managers felt that by the end of the decade, meetings with ministers and civil servants had a different atmosphere. There was less reliance on external expertise and less sympathy for views that might question preferred policies. Child care had also become more political in a way that it had not been before; indeed, in 1948 a gentleman's agreement was negotiated with other government departments by the Home Office (then responsible for children in care), that child welfare be kept out of party politics.

Despite these struggles, BAAF's initial vision that it should build on the strengths which it had inherited was quickly realised in that early period and the organisation achieved a reputation for sound cross-disciplinary research,

policy and practice advice, and training. It caught the ear of those involved at all layers – from government ministers to social workers, doctors, lawyers and foster carers and adopters. There was also an important administrative and financial need to maintain previous levels of membership, particularly as the number of voluntary adoption agencies was declining.

By 1986, BAAF had grown beyond recognition with a budget (one million pounds) ten times larger than in 1978. All local authorities and voluntary adoption agencies were still in membership, active and influential legal, medical and black perspective groups were in place, *Be My Parent* and the adoption exchange were doing well (the 2,000th placement was achieved in 1985), local and national advertising of children was successfully established and personalities, including Bob Monkhouse and footballer John Fashanu, gave their support to the organisation's policies. In addition, real change had been achieved in the definition of special needs children, with no child or family group regarded as unplaceable in a permanent family. Huge efforts had been made to find black families for black children, so exploding the myth that black families do not adopt; the concept of permanence was part of social work thinking; there were effective arrangements for handling the press and media; a set of authoritative publications had emerged and the need for clear decision-making on children's futures was better acknowledged, despite continuing practice shortcomings.

There are dilemmas facing all charities in that the vigorous pursuit of policies can sometimes undermine scientific rigour and objective standing. This is often counterproductive when public suspicion of exaggeration leads people to think that the problem does not actually exist. In those early years, BAAF took a cautious but cumulative approach, remaining strongly focused and active on specific issues, not growing too fast, establishing an interdisciplinary ethos and treading a delicate path with governments, while remaining credible to them.

The 1990s

In the early 1990s, new projects were undertaken and specific political issues continued to arise. For example, after the fall of Communism and the Balkan wars in the 1990s, there was a need to help children who had been brought up in dreadful institutions. BAAF's policy was to do as much as possible to help reform domestic systems, for example, by providing training and advice in Kosovo. Similarly, on the home front, an unanticipated debate flared up about the use of single people as adopters. In addition, by the middle of the decade, there were financial difficulties and something of a crisis of confidence in BAAF, including the loss of a number of local authority members.

In the midst of these problems, Felicity Collier was appointed Director in 1995. She had worked in child care social work and family court welfare and, latterly, as an Assistant Director of Probation in Oxfordshire where one of her responsibilities was young offender institutions. This desire to improve outcomes for children in care, a sizeable proportion of whom went on to prison custody, and her experience as a senior manager led her to apply for the directorship (retitled Chief Executive from 1997).

Felicity's initial aim was to restore confidence in BAAF as an organisation that could make a real difference to children and provide services to members, which were perceived as essential for good practice and giving value for money. In recognition of the growing number of individual members (as opposed to agencies), the name was changed again in 2001 to the British *Association* for Adoption and Fostering. In addition to restoring BAAF's stability, she led the expansion of its range of services, including a carefully planned conference and training programme backed by a range of authoritative publications and a modular qualification system. Specialist social work and research groups were established to join the flourishing legal, medical and black perspectives advisory groups and the board of trustees was trimmed and reappointed to make it more representative of members' interests and able to give effective governance. In 2000, John Simmonds, an academic and trainer from Goldsmiths College, was also appointed Head of Policy, Research and Development to strengthen the management team.

Alongside these organisational reforms, controversial issues and the Government's hostility to what was seen as a 'politically correct organisational culture' had to be addressed. Especially salient among these were intercountry adoptions, the emergence of independent fostering organisations and the suggestion that children whose single mothers could not support them should be compulsorily adopted.

With regard to intercountry adoptions, Felicity was concerned to move the organisation from the oppositional stance it had taken in the past while recognising that intercountry adoption was not a solution for the thousands of children living in poverty across the world. There was additional work to ensure that when it did occur, it met legal and human rights conditions. Training and advice were also offered to the sending countries to help them improve their own services.

The growth of independent fostering organisations posed a more serious ideological challenge. The principle of fostering for profit jarred with BAAF's core beliefs and there was a fear that, if invited to join BAAF, the organisations would use their membership status to convey professional approval. BAAF therefore campaigned for registration and inspection and set up a forum for the promotion of good practice and exchange of ideas.

The proposal on compulsory adoption coincided with a fall in the number of available babies, reflecting sympathetic attitudes to single parenthood and abortion. To deal with this, the founding principle that BAAF was primarily a service for children was evoked and a coalition of like-minded organisations formed to influence pending legislation. This led to the widely supported statement, *Adoption: Myths and realities* (ADSS/BAAF, 2000).

Throughout this period, there was growing concern about abuse in substitute care and horrific revelations of events, especially in residential care. But foster and adoptive homes were not immune from suspicion and BAAF found itself giving a considerable amount of advice to its members to deal with these problems and encouraged the Government to increase police checks and other safeguarding devices.

By 1997, the Conservative Government had been in power for 18 years and appeared to be running out of steam. Although they had been careful with public money, children's services had fared relatively well and its Children Act 1989 was a landmark of reform. The Act said little about adoption but it freed foster care from the shackles of less eligibility by acknowledging its place in the spectrum of services and giving social workers more freedom to provide whatever they deemed appropriate for a child in need.

Later that year, the Government changed and children became an integral part of New Labour thinking. There was a sharp focus on disadvantaged groups, in which looked after children commanded a high profile. In particular, there was a review of adoption ordered by the Prime Minister himself (Performance and Innovation Unit, 2000). BAAF's proposal for a national adoption register, modelled on its successful BAAFLink service, was endorsed and although the initial contract to run this was placed elsewhere, it was awarded to BAAF in 2004 and grew into an effective service. This complemented the *Be My Parent* family-finding service, a development from the earlier 'exchange' system, which itself was expanded to provide a monthly, later colour, newspaper and which is now also online.

Another important part of Labour's child care policy was to increase the number of adoptions from care. This resulted from evidence that hopes to reunify many children with their birth families had proved too optimistic, by which time their age and experiences of changes of carers and other adverse circumstances made them more difficult to place. There was also a growing voice of people whose applications to adopt had been rejected without appeal. The Government introduced the Independent Review Mechanism (IRM), which BAAF successfully tendered to operate.

Finally, a significant legacy of this period was the adoption statistics research project. Prior to 1996, there was a dearth of information about adoption – the children, the adopters, the agencies, etc. Funding was secured from the Department of Health for a substantial project which provided details on 95 per cent of children adopted from care (Ivaldi, 2000). The results were highly significant as they showed that the majority of children later adopted had entered care as infants, had never been returned home and had experienced several changes of carer. Black and mixed heritage children, siblings and disabled children were the most poorly served. Given the more sympathetic political climate, BAAF campaigned successfully to introduce features now accepted as the infrastructure of family placement, namely:

• appropriate legislation;

• national adoption standards;

• early care planning;

• monitoring of permanency plans;

• a national adoption register;

• mandatory assessment for adoption support;

• parental leave for adoptive parents;

• the acceptance of unmarried and same-sex adopters;

• access to an intermediary service for birth parents trying to gain non-identifying information on their adult adopted children;

• tighter legislation on private fostering.

One major disappointment was that while the Adoption Support Regulations introduced the right to an adoption support assessment and plan, it did not require the local authority to provide those services.

With a more sympathetic government in power, the issue of how far BAAF should maintain its independence, as opposed to becoming a quasi-governmental agency, resurfaced. Tony Hall's original stance was vindicated in that it was agreed that relevant contracts had to be tendered for if BAAF was to play its part in improving services for children, but the stance should be that of a 'a government's critical friend', with activities where BAAF's voice was constrained tightly ring fenced.

Felicity Collier stayed until 2006 and throughout her directorship was fortunate to be well supported by the Chairs of BAAF. Terry Connor, Director of a leading Catholic adoption agency, was responsible for her appointment; Ian Sparks, Chief Executive of The Children's Society and with a financial services background, held the post from 1996 and Sir Edward Cazalet, a newly retired judge in the Family Division of the High Court and a skilled fundraiser, was Chair from 2000 until 2003. He was followed by Anthony Douglas, a local authority children's services director and, since 2004, Chief Executive of CAFCASS, who is still Chair today. An indication of BAAF's successes after 1997 was the size of the annual turnover, which had grown threefold to almost six million pounds by 2005. There was also 100 per cent local authority membership across the UK – no mean achievement given that local government in the UK had been reorganised between 1996 and 1998, creating over 40 more potential members.

The past decade
David Holmes became Chief Executive of BAAF in early 2006. A solicitor by background, he was the lead official on the Adoption and Children Bill as it made its passage through Parliament and also managed the national implementation programme for the new legislation from 2002 to 2005. David joined BAAF because of the charity's success in finding permanent new families for looked after children and its ability directly to influence relevant policy and practice through its publications, training, project and lobbying work.

Under David's leadership, recent years have seen BAAF continue to concentrate on the delivery of its core values and beliefs in promoting permanency planning and permanent solutions for children separated from their parents. In doing so, it has also focused on the importance of solutions other than adoption – particularly family and friends care and foster care and, of course, returning children to their parents wherever possible. As a membership organisation, particularly unusual in professional social work practice, BAAF's history marks out the importance and contribution that inter-professional co-operation and perspectives can make to meeting the needs of children separated from their parents and families.

The multi-disciplinary focus of BAAF is also unique. Social work, health and law were at the cornerstone of its activities from the start, added to by black and minority ethnic perspectives and, in the last ten years, the research community. Education is and continues to be the one missing element of membership, although various initiatives, such as Kate Cairns's *Learn the Child* (2004), a special edition of this journal edited by Sonia Jackson (2007) and the *Supporting Children's Learning* training programme (Pallett *et al*, 2010), indicate some progress.

An extremely significant feature of the last decade has been the impact of devolution on the development of child care policy in the UK and in 2006 BAAF opened an office in Northern Ireland to join the existing eight offices in England, Wales and Scotland. Links with the four governments and Parliaments continue to be equally important, the significance of which is clearly emerging in the different policy contexts across the UK.

While the focus of policy for children 'in care' across the four UK countries remains broadly similar in objectives and principles, particularly the welfare of the child, there is no denying that the different legal frameworks and systems, and policy initiatives, are introducing divergence and diversity that make day-to-day practice across these countries all the more challenging. This has been especially so with different timetables for the modernisation of adoption legislation in England and Wales, Scotland and Northern Ireland. The availability of different legal orders marks some of that divergence with special guardianship in England and Wales and the permanence order in Scotland. Northern Ireland still awaits its new legislation. These orders provided different solutions to similar kinds of problems and only in time will we discover their relative merits in relation to the children whose lives they will affect. Divergence can also be found in the use of residential care, family and friends care and responses to juvenile offending.

Developments in fostering have been equally significant, with concerns about the recruitment and retention of carers, the 'professionalisation debate', the contribution of the independent sector and the importance of a recognised skills and knowledge framework including those required for specific interventions and treatments. Again, the four countries have their own important perspectives on these issues. Other divergences will be found in the organisational structure in the delivery of services such as children's services in England, combining social services and education, and the Health and Social Care Boards in Northern Ireland.

What does remain coherent across all four countries is a belief in the importance of adoption as a permanent solution for children who cannot return to their birth parents or families. Whatever differences might be found in the detail and whatever debates there continue to

be about human rights questions, there is nothing to suggest that any of the four countries have moved away from that belief and a legal and policy framework that supports it. Where there is a notable divergence is the difference in position between UK countries and Europe over the use of adoption. In most of Europe adoption is focused on – and indeed means – intercountry adoption. Conversely, as we have seen, intercountry adoption in the UK has been viewed with considerable ambivalence under the anxiety of its colonial past, significant anxieties about transracial placements and a belief in the importance of services being developed locally to preserve the nationality and identity of families and children. Most European countries, where the human rights issues associated with legally severing a child from its family of origin against the wishes of the parents are barely even an issue, do not share this perspective on the advantages of domestic adoption in relation to children in state care. This reminds us that ethics and law are as important as a child's needs and development, and the ways in which these are worked out in the creation of a nation's child care policy has profound consequences.

This specific divergence is not confined to adoption. Lessons from Europe have not been particularly significant to the UK, although there has been some interest in the advantages of Scandinavian approaches to child welfare, and the contribution that the North European tradition of social pedagogy might make to the over-bureaucratised, risk-adverse and impersonal approaches to working directly with children. Neither has Europe been particularly interested in lessons from the UK, although attachment, especially Schofield and Beek's *The Attachment Handbook* (2006), has excited interest in Scandinavia. A French translation is also close to agreement and other BAAF books have appeared in a variety of languages. The extent of influence is somewhat different in the accession countries, with BAAF making direct contributions to the development of adoption and fostering services in Romania, Serbia and the Czech Republic.

Family-finding in both adoption and permanent foster care remains at the heart of BAAF's services. The contract to run the Adoption Register in England and Wales became a significant addition to BAAF's role in family placement and now finds families for someone in four of the children referred to it. In 2010, the Adoption Regional Information System (ARIS) was launched in Northern Ireland, incorporating a database that will provide agencies with centralised information about children waiting for an adoptive family and waiting adopters. In addition, BAAF has contracts to manage family-finding consortia in Wales and Scotland. The benefits of modern technology have also led to the establishment of *Be My Parent* as an online service as well as the development of video profiling, with the 'Opening Doors' project using it to overcome the limitations of written profiles of children, especially where they are disabled. The advantages of doing this were quickly established and funding allowed for a new video research project to be created for nearly 70 children, more than half of whom went on to be placed within the duration of the project (BAAF, 2010a). The Adoption, Search and Reunion website (BAAF, 2010b) is another example.

The opportunities that BAAF creates for the professional exchange of information among peers, and the opportunity to reflect and learn from experience and to understand the needs of practitioners, have led to a number of important research projects based on BAAF's partnerships with leading UK universities: 'Permanency in Foster Care' led by Gill Schofield at the University of East Anglia; the British Chinese Adoption project led by Alan Rushton at Kings College, London; and 'Unaccompanied Asylum Seeking Young People in Foster Care' led by Jim Wade at York University and Ravi Kohli at the University of Bedfordshire – to name just a few. Other developments are internally generated and often initiated by advisory groups themselves; BAAF's health forms, its Guidance on genetic testing and obesity, and Mather and colleagues' *Doctors for Children in Public Care* (2000) are important examples.

A significant part of the organisation's direct influence has stemmed from the extensive commitment it has made to providing training, consultancy and education. BAAF trainer/consultants provided some 2,500 days of training across the UK in 2009 and chaired over 30 adoption and fostering panels. The first PQ course in advanced child care came about through a BAAF initiative and Margaret Adcock's link with Goldsmiths College in the early 1980s. In recent years, under the leadership of Barbara Hutchinson, BAAF's recently retired Executive Director, the organisation has developed its post-qualifying training to offer a degree level GSCC-validated PQ course in Safeguarding and Family Placement, in partnership with Sheffield Hallam University in England and equivalents in Scotland and Northern Ireland and, at the planning stage, in Wales. BAAF also brings a multi-disciplinary audience together at more than 20 conferences a year. *Adoption & Fostering* is an internationally recognised peer-reviewed journal.

Campaigning and media work are another major part of BAAF's responsibilities – November 2010 marks the 14th year of National Adoption Week, bringing to wide public attention the value and significance of adoption generally and, specifically, the needs of children profiled throughout the week itself.

In 2009/10 BAAF's turnover was close to £7.5 million – the highest ever. There were some 2,000 corporate and individual members including every local authority (Trusts in Northern Ireland) across the UK. The vast majority of voluntary adoption agencies and independent fostering providers are in membership and BAAF operates a range of thriving special interest groups on subjects of particular interest, such as special guardianship and private fostering. The latter deserves a special mention being a subject of significant concern to BAAF for many years. Government funding was made available to develop a series of awareness-raising campaigns, and the available evidence suggests this has led to a significant increase in understanding among professionals and the general public.

Looking to the future

As BAAF celebrates its 30th anniversary, it is clear that that there is much to acknowledge and celebrate. But while a sense of achievement is appropriate, there is also cause for both regret and real concern. There remains widespread concern about the position of children in society. Social and economic inequality is still marked and where a child is born and the social and economic position of their parents still too often determines their life chances and pathways. This is not to say that things have not changed, as demonstrated by the recent report on equality (Equality and Human Rights Commission, 2010), but as *The Spirit Level* (Wilkinson and Pickett, 2009) has also shown, society is structurally stuck in perpetuating gross inequalities and a context less sympathetic to minorities and vulnerable groups. This is, of course, a matter beyond social work, although in the 1970s many social workers would have seen it as a matter of direct, primary professional concern. Political activism has largely evaporated from social work but the consequences of political decisions reverberate on those with whom social workers are most concerned. For children on the edge of care or in care, social inequality plus maltreatment creates serious developmental consequences. Direct abuse or toxic neglect, together with parental drug and alcohol misuse, mental health problems, domestic violence and learning difficulties have profound consequences for children and are at the core of family placement work. The impact and consequences of these issues on assessment, planning and decision-making and family placement need knowledge, skill and resources. They require health, education and social

work to work together with carers and adopters, often in the long term. A loving, stable, resourceful and determined family for life has been BAAF's key message over 30 years and that remains unchanged. But the full meaning of what it demands and how it might be enabled in the current context is quite different from the past, both at the individual child level in relation to their needs, and in the general population in terms of those families most at risk. The demand on the system as a whole is enormous in understanding and properly addressing these issues. But whatever demands there are on professionals, it is the children and their adopters, foster carers or carers who carry the 24/7 weight of responsibility. The public image of social workers and the care system as a whole does not help. While BAAF continues to support and develop best practice and expends a lot of energy in presenting a more accurate and positive picture of social work and care, there are complex systemic and structural forces at work which have made this an uphill battle and one that does not seem to get much easier. There are also continuing concerns about delay for all children in care, and about the non-delivery of adoption plans or other permanent options for a significant number of children. There is further serious anxiety about the identification of effective interventions and the availability of support services in health, mental health and education to manage effectively the consequences of maltreatment. Building this into the placement from the start and making it available as the child and family develop still tend to happen according to a postcode lottery. Adequately addressing the issues for young people leaving care also makes frustratingly slow progress.

As a professional membership organisation, BAAF is as much needed today as it was 30 years ago. But as has happened over those three decades, it has had to develop and respond to changing circumstances and demonstrate its worth for the investment made by those who provide the resources for BAAF's work. As this article is written, deep cuts are being planned in public funding which will impact on all of BAAF's stakeholders. The organisation is having to ride a wave of uncertainty about its future. At the same time, the demands on services from local authorities, the voluntary sector and the courts are rising. The numbers and complexity of the issues presented to BAAF's information and advice service are also increasing.

BAAF will continue to work with its professional membership to address these complex issues as it always has done. It will not lose its primary focus on those children who are most vulnerable in society – those who are permanently or temporarily separated from their families of origin and those who care for them. It will undoubtedly have to adapt to survive. But the needs of professionals working with those children and carers have not lessened; this was the motivation for creating BAAF and this is the need that exists for such work to continue. Whether through its publications or advice lines, its policy work or campaigns, its training or its family-finding, the work goes on. The organisation is a home for professional practice in family placement and a secure and loving home is what we all need.

Happy 30th Birthday BAAF!

References

Adcock M and White R, 'Adoption, custodianship or fostering?', *Adoption & Fostering* 9:4, pp 14–18, 1985

ADSS/BAAF, *Adoption: Myths and reality*, London: ADSS, 2000

BAAF, *Seeing the Difference? Using video clips to help find families for children*, London: BAAF, 2010a

BAAF, *Adoption, Search and Reunion*, website, 2010b; www.adoptionsearchandreunion.org.uk

Cairns K, *Learn the Child*, London: BAAF, 2004

Equality and Human Rights Commission, *How Fair is Britain?*, 2010; retrieved 22 October 2010, from www.equalityhumanrights.com/key-projects/triennial-review/

Gill O and Jackson B, *Adoption and Race*, London: BAAF/Batsford, 1983

Hall A, *The Point of Entry: Study of client reception in the social services*, London: Allen & Unwin, 1975

Hazel N, *A Bridge to Independence*, Oxford: Basil Blackwell, 1981

Ivaldi G, *Surveying Adoption: A comprehensive analysis of local authority adoptions 1998–9*, London: BAAF, 2000

Jackson S (ed), *Adoption & Fostering: Education*, Special Edition, 2007

Masson JM, Norbury D and Chatterton SG, *Mine, Yours or Ours? A study of step-parent adoption*, London: HMSO, 1983

Mather M, Batty D and Payne H, *Doctors for Children in Public Care*, London: BAAF, 2000

Pallett C, Simmonds J and Warman A, *Supporting Children's Learning*, London: BAAF, 2010

Parker R, *Caring for Separated Children*, London: MacMillan, 1980

Performance and Innovation Unit, *Prime Minister's Review of Adoption*, London: The Cabinet Office, 2000

Rowe J and Lambert L, *Children who Wait*, London: ABAFA, 1973

Rowe J, Cain H, Hundleby M and Keane A, *Long-term Foster Care*, London: Batsford, 1984

Schofield G and Beek M, *The Attachment Handbook*, London: BAAF, 2006

Seebohm (Chair), *Report by the Committee on Local Authority and Allied Social Services*, London: HMSO, 1968

Short (Chair), *Report of the House of Commons Social Services Committee on Children in Care*, London: HMSO, 1984

Triseliotis J and Russell J, *Hard to Place: The outcome of adoption and residential care*, London: Heinemann, 1984

Wilkinson R and Pickett K, *The Spirit Level: Why more equal societies almost always do better*, London: Allen Lane, 2009

Legal notes

England and Wales

Leave to remove the child from the jurisdiction pending a Convention adoption application

Essex County Council v SM & others
High Court Family Division (Hedley J)
14 July 2010 [2010] EWHCA 1694

S was a seven-year-old child whose parents had accepted that they were unable to care for her. Her paternal aunt and uncle, who lived in the USA, were put forward as carers and were assessed by US authorities as appropriate adopters. The plan was for S to move to to the US to live with her aunt and uncle for a period of at least ten weeks, after which they would return to England and apply for a Convention adoption in the English courts. The local authority applied for a placement order and for leave under section 28 of the Adoption and Children Act 2002 to remove the child from the jurisdiction.

Held
Although the making of a placement order conferred parental responsibility on the prospective adopters, under section 25(3) S's aunt and uncle would remain prohibited from taking her to the US for the purposes of adoption by section 85. This allows a child to be removed from the jurisdiction for the purposes of adoption only where parental responsibility has been granted under section 84. Hedley J ruled that section 85 should be interpreted as covering only permanent removals for the purpose of adoption abroad. As this case concerned a prospective Convention adoption in England, as required by the US immigration authorities, the removal of S from England would be temporary only. The court suggests that it should be clearly stated that the child

Alexandra Conroy Harris, BAAF's Legal Consultant, prepared these notes

remains subject to the English jurisdiction, permission to remove should be given for a fixed period of time and the prospective adopters should give an undertaking to return the child to the jurisdiction at the end of that period, or earlier if so required.

Comment
This is an interesting alternative approach to the difficulties of reconciling the restrictions of section 85 with the requirement of section 42 that the child live with the adopters for ten weeks before an application for adoption can be made. In the previously reported case, *Re A* [2009] EWCA Civ 41, the child had not been matched with the adopters and the placement was for the purpose of assessment. The care order was still active and leave of the court for removal from the jurisdiction under paragraph 19 of Schedule 2 of the Children Act 1989 was required. In this case the placement order had suspended the care order and Schedule 2 did not apply.

Meaning of 'couple' for the purpose of adoption

T & M v OCC & C
High Court Family Division (Hedley J)
13 May 2010 [2010] EWHCA 964

T and M are a lesbian couple who lived for a time in Nicaragua. While there they adopted two children, J and C, but as the law of Nicaragua did not allow joint adoption of children by same-sex couples, T adopted J, who had spent her life in an orphanage, and M adopted C, a member of M's extended family. The family later moved to England and are now all British citizens. As a result of her early experiences, J developed an attachment disorder which created difficulties in her relationship with M. M and T decided that the best way to preserve the stability of the family was to live in separate but nearby houses. J lives with T and C divides her time between the houses. The adults see each other every day and the family spend

Alexandra Plumtree,
Legal Consultant at
BAAF's Scottish
Centre, prepared
these notes

time together at weekends and on shared holidays. C regards both T and M as her parents.

M and T applied jointly to adopt C on the basis that M was C's sole legal parent since the adoption in Nicaragua.

As Nicaragua was neither a Hague Convention country nor on the Designated list, C's adoption was not recognised in the UK and the court would need to recognise it as an adoption at common law before M could consent to a further adoption. If that was possible, the court then had to decide whether M and T were a couple who could adopt within the meaning of section 50 of the Adoption and Children Act 2002.

Held

After obtaining expert advice on the status of adoption in Nicaragua and the validity of the order obtained, Hedley J was satisfied that he could make a declaration that the adoption was valid and that M was the mother and sole legal parent of C. He then considered the meaning of the definition of a couple as two people 'living as partners in an enduring family relationship' and was satisfied that M and T had an 'unambiguous intention to create and maintain family life' and had set up their living arrangements to be consistent with that intention. He therefore found that M and T were eligible jointly to adopt C.

Comment

The facts of this case are highly unlikely to be duplicated, but are reported here as an example of the court's willingness to accept less conventional family arrangements as providing a suitable framework for the adoption of a child.

Scotland[1]

Child care law: relationship between children's hearing system and private law

Knox v S and the Lord Advocate; and L v Ritchie and the Lord Advocate
Court of Session, Scotland
Extra Division: Lord Kingarth, Lord Clarke and Lord Mackay of Drumadoon
26 May 2010

These were two separate appeals which were dealt with together by the court because they both raised the same issue: whether an unmarried father with a contact order under section 11 of the Children (Scotland) Act 1995 was a 'relevant person' for the purposes of proceedings in the children's hearing system, in terms of section 93(2)(b) of the 1995 Act. 'Relevant person' status in the hearing system gives the person the right to be invited to and attend all hearings, to receive all papers, to be represented at hearings, and to appeal against hearing decisions.

In the first case, *Knox v S and the Lord Advocate*, S was the unmarried father of TQ, who was aged three at the time of the judgment. The mother acknowledged S as TQ's father, but he was not named on the birth certificate and did not have parental responsibilities and rights. He had some contact with TQ in 2007. He applied to the sheriff court for various orders under section 11 of the 1995 Act, and while that application was proceeding, he was granted a contact order on 21 February 2008. In January 2008, TQ was referred to a children's hearing, and grounds relating to a lack of parental care on the part of his mother were established on 8 February 2008. S maintained he did not know about the hearing proceedings. A

---

[1] All cases are available on the Scottish courts website: www.scotcourts.gov.uk.

supervision requirement was made on 19 March 2008, with a condition that TQ should have no contact with his father. S was not invited to or notified about the hearing and received no papers, and the hearing proceeded on the basis that he was not a 'relevant person'.

When S learned about the hearing proceedings, he asked for interim parental responsibilities and rights under section 11 of the 1995 Act, but this was refused by the sheriff on 7 April 2008. In addition, S appealed against the hearing decision of 19 March, particularly against the refusal to treat him as a 'relevant person'. The sheriff granted S's appeal and held that he was a relevant person. The reporter appealed against that decision to the Court of Session.

In the second case, *L v Ritchie and the Lord Advocate*, L was the unmarried father of MF, who was eleven at the time of the judgment. He was acknowledged as the father and named on the birth certificate. However, L did not have parental responsibilities and rights in terms of section 3 of the 1995 Act, as amended with effect from 4 May 2006 by section 23 of the Family Law (Scotland) Act 2006, because MF was born before that date. On 12 April 2002, L was granted a contact order under section 11 of the 1995 Act, and exercised contact until May 2008, when the mother stopped it. MF was referred to a children's hearing and a supervision requirement was made on 9 October 2008, with a condition that MF have no contact with his father. L was invited to attend the hearing, but was not given 'relevant person' status. He received no papers, was excluded from part of the hearing, was not given information about the grounds for referral and did not receive a copy of the reasons for the decision that MF should have no contact with him.

L appealed against the hearing decision of 9 October, particularly against the refusal to treat him as a 'relevant person'. The sheriff refused L's appeal and held that he was not a 'relevant person'. L appealed against that decision to the Court of Session.

Held

That the sheriff in the first case was correct and in the second case was incorrect, and that S and L were relevant persons in the respective children's hearing proceedings.

The judgment of the court was give by Lord Kingarth. He set out the factual background to the cases and the legislative framework of the 1995 Act, both the private law provisions in Part I (particularly sections 1–3 and 11) and the children's hearing provisions in Chapters 2 and 3 of Part II. He outlined the definition of 'relevant person' in section 93(2)(b) of the 1995 Act, the rights given to a 'relevant person', and other rights available to someone who is not a 'relevant person'.

The judgment also set out the legal arguments presented on behalf of the children's reporters, the two fathers and the Lord Advocate. The Lord Advocate had become a party to the appeals, particularly because they raised issues under the European Convention on Human Rights (ECHR) and the Human Rights Act 1998. One of the issues for the appeal court was whether the definition of 'relevant person' in section 93(2)(b) of the 1995 Act was compatible with the ECHR, and if not, whether there should be a declaration of incompatibility.

The submissions for the children's reporters were that the scheme of the 1995 Act was not incompatible with Article 6 (right to a fair hearing) or Article 8 (right to respect for family life) of the ECHR and that the proper interpretation of section 93(2)(b) did not include a parent with a contact order. The submissions for S and L were that a proper reading of the definition of 'relevant person' must include a father with a contact order. If S and L were not considered to be relevant persons, that would not be compatible with their rights under Articles 6 and 8. The position of the Lord Advocate was that there should be no declaration of incompatibility, and that the children reporters' interpretation of section 93(2)(b) was the correct one.

The decision of the court was that there was an incompatibility between the 1995 Act and Article 6 of the ECHR. However, the 1995 Act could be construed so as to avoid that incompatibility. The definition of 'relevant person' in section 93(2)(b)(a) should be read as 'Any parent enjoying parental responsibilities or parental rights *or a right of contact in terms of a contact order* under Part I of this Act' [emphasis added to show the additional words]. S and L should therefore be treated as a 'relevant person' in their respective children's hearing proceedings.

The appeal court distinguished or differentiated the cases of S and L from the decision in *Principal Reporter v K* 2010 SLT 308, previously reported in *Adoption & Fostering* (34:1, 2010, p 82). In that case, the appeal court had taken the view that the unmarried father was not a 'relevant person', because he had no contact order, although he had a pending court application for various orders under section 11 of the 1995 Act.

Note

This case changes the wording of section 93(2)(b)(a) of the 1995 Act, with the inclusion of the words highlighted. Any father who does not have responsibilities and/or rights but does have a contact order under section 11 of the 1995 Act must now be treated as a 'relevant person' for the purposes of children's hearings.

Cases in brief

Permanence order: whether variation of supervision requirement should be allowed

City of Edinburgh Council, Petitioners, in respect of CM
Sheriffdom of Lothian and Borders at Edinburgh
Sheriff KEC Mackie
9 April 2010

This was an application for a permanence order with authority for adoption for the child CM. While the case was pending, the local authority asked the children's hearing to vary CM's supervision requirement, to allow his place of residence to be changed to new carers who were to be prospective adopters. The hearing was in favour of varying the supervision requirement and prepared a report to this effect under section 95 of the Adoption and Children (Scotland) Act 2007, asking the court to refer the case to them for the variation, under section 96. The sheriff refused to allow the variation, and discussed some of the difficulties which have arisen with that section.

Permanence order: which welfare test applies and whether Devolution issue arises

City of Edinburgh Council, Petitioners, in respect of CM
Sheriffdom of Lothian and Borders at Edinburgh
Sheriff KEC Mackie
1 July 2010

In the same application as above, for a permanence order with authority for adoption for CM, the agent for a birth parent raised a Devolution issue about the different welfare tests for courts considering such cases under the Adoption and Children (Scotland) Act 2007. The welfare test in adoption applications is in section 14, and the test is the welfare of the child throughout life. The welfare test in permanence order applications is in section 84 and the test is the welfare of the child throughout childhood, that is until the age of 18. The sheriff held that no Devolution issue arose and that both sections applied for different parts of the decision, when the application was for a permanence order for authority for adoption.

Permanence order: whether parental consent to adoption should be dispensed with

East Lothian Council, Petitioners, in respect of LK
Sheriffdom of Lothian and Borders at Haddington
Sheriff Peter Gillam
30 July 2010

This was an application for a permanence order with authority for adoption for LK. It was opposed by the birth parents. Sheriff Gillam heard evidence and considered the case. He granted the permanence order with authority for adoption and with various ancillary provisions, allowed some indirect contact, dispensed with the consent of the birth parents under section 83 of the Adoption and Children (Scotland) Act 2007 and terminated LK's supervision requirement. (This case is under appeal.)

Brief notes

1. Adoption and Children (Scotland) Act 2007

As reported in previous Notes, secondary legislation is still awaited to ensure that provisions in England, Wales and Northern Ireland take account of and recognise the 2007 Act. In the meantime, two further orders have been made relating to, although not wholly concerned with, the 2007 Act:

• Parental Responsibility and Measures for the Protection of Children (International Obligations) (Scotland) Regulations 2010, SSI 2010/213. These are to implement international obligations, but they affect permanence order applications if there are jurisdiction issues around claims from other contracting countries.

• Rehabilitation of Offenders Act 1974 (Exclusions and Exceptions)(Scotland) Amendment Order 2010, SSI 2010/243. This amends the Rehabilitation of Offenders Act 1974 (Exclusions and Exceptions)(Scotland) Amendment Order

2003, SSI 2003/231, as already amended, and among other things Article 6 makes changes consequent on the 2007 Act. This order comes into force on the same day as section 91 of the Protection of Vulnerable Groups (Scotland) Act 2007.

These Scottish regulations can be found under their individual number at www.uk-legislation.hmso.gov.uk/legislation/scotland/s-stat. From August 2010, the OPSI/HMSO website is being replaced by www.legislation.gov.uk managed by the National Archives, although the OPSI pages are still available.

Practice Notes for all Sheriffdoms for proceedings under the 2007 Act are now on the Scottish courts website www.scotcourts.gov.uk under Sheriff Court Practice Notes for 2009.

2. Children's hearing system reform

Stage 2 consideration of the Bill started on 15 September, with detailed line-by-line consideration. The deadline for completion of Stage 2 is 29 October. The full text of the Bill, written and oral evidence, the Stage 1 Report and supporting documentation are available on www.scottish.parliament.uk under Current Bills. There is also background information on the Scottish Government website www.scotland.gov.uk; click on Topics, People and Society, Young People and Children's Hearings System Reform.

3. Protection of Vulnerable Groups (Scotland) Act 2007

The Protecting Vulnerable Groups (PVG) Scheme will be brought into force on 30 November 2010. It will replace and improve the current disclosure arrangements for people who work with vulnerable groups, including children. The latest 'Special Issue' Newsletter, 28 June 2010, is available on the Scottish Government website, www.scotland.gov.uk under Topics, People and Society, Young People, Support for

Children and Families, Protecting Vulnerable Groups Scheme. There is also a list of secondary legislation at the same web address; click on PVG Secondary Legislation.

4. Registration and inspection regimes for children's services

Implementation of the Public Services Reform (Scotland) Act 2010 is still anticipated on 1 April 2011, changing the roles and names of the registration and inspection systems for child care services, among others. Two orders have been made to enable implementation work and the making of regulations, etc, the Public Services Reform (Scotland) (Commencement No. 1) and (Commencement No. 2) Orders, SSI 2010/221 and 321 respectively. The Scottish Government have issued a Consultation paper on regulations, for response by 5 November. This is available on their website under Publications, 10 September 2010. Other implementation information is available on the same website under Topics, Health and Community Care, Improvement and Scrutiny.

5. Current Bills

These Scottish Bills are available at www.scottish.parliament.uk the Scottish Parliament's website under 'Current Bills' and the name of the specific Bill.

(a) Criminal Justice and Licensing (Scotland) Act 2010

This was passed on 30 June and received the Royal Assent on 6 August 2010. Among many other provisions, section 52 raises the age at which a child may be prosecuted, from eight to 12. This is done by inserting a new section 41A into the Criminal Procedure (Scotland) Act 1995

(b) Children's Hearings (Scotland) Bill

See 2 above.

(c) Autism (Scotland) Bill

This is a Member's Bill, introduced on 26 May 2010, to impose a duty on the Scottish Ministers to publish an autism strategy. The strategy is one for meeting the needs of children and adults in Scotland with autistic spectrum conditions. The lead committee for Stage 1 is the Education, Lifelong Learning and Culture Committee, which asked for written evidence by 8 October and will take oral evidence in November. Stage 1 is due to be completed by 21 January 2011.

(d) Commissioner for Victims and Witnesses (Scotland) Bill

This is a Member's Bill, introduced on 27 May 2010. It is intended 'to provide for the establishment and functions of a Commissioner for Victims and Witnesses; and for connected purposes'. The lead Committee for Stage 1 is the Justice Committee, which asked for written evidence by 24 September and hopes to hear oral evidence later in the year.

Northern Ireland

Kerry O'Halloran, lawyer, social worker and Adjunct Professor at the Centre of Philanthropy and Non-profit Studies, QUT, Brisbane, prepared these notes

Article 50 of the Children (Northern Ireland) Order 1995: significant harm; onus on Trust to establish, on the balance of probability, its case that an account of non-accidental injury was not correct

In the Matter of KW, EW & MW between HSC Trust and SM & EW
The High Court (Weir J)
Delivered 28 June 2010

This case concerned an application from a Trust for a determination of the issue as to whether non-accidental injuries sustained by EW were deliberately inflicted.

Background

The relationship between SM, the mother, and EW senior (EWS) – the parents of KW, EW and MW – commenced in 2003 and was from the outset characterised by excessive alcohol misuse by EWS leading to verbal and physical altercations. KW was born in July 2004 and there were two respite placements in the summer of 2005 as a result of concerns regarding the parents' lifestyle. EW was born in October 2005 and although SM struggled to care for both children, further respite care for KW was required in November and later that month, again due to problems between the parents, EW had to be voluntarily accommodated in a respite placement. Attempts were made to rehabilitate the children to their parents' care by means of residential assessments but these proved unsuccessful due to SM's inability to cope with the children and EWS's continued misuse of alcohol. The two children, therefore, returned to foster care and care orders in respect of both of them were granted in May 2007. The then care plan was for permanency by adoption.

In February 2008, SM gave birth to a third child, MW, and embarked upon a PACT assessment that proved successful and enabled SM and MW to live together in the community. An intensive support package was made available and SM is reported to have engaged well with the services provided. By May 2009, matters had progressed to a point at which MW's name could be removed from the Child Protection Register and a decision was further taken to revisit the Trust's care plan for KW and EW. SM indicated that she would like to have both children returned to her care and EWS agreed with this and advised that he would be willing to offer ongoing support.

Accordingly, in July 2009, SM embarked upon a placement at a Family Centre initially with MW and subsequently with KW and EW. The assessment was successfully completed in September 2009 and SM returned to the community with all three children. SM relates that matters progressed well in the family centre but began to deteriorate upon her return to the community. The support promised by EWS did not materialise. He was not particularly involved in caring for the children, was not supportive for the most part and frequently would not get out of bed until midday. She was the person with responsibility for caring for the children at all times. She describes becoming more and more drained as the weeks went on and trying to explain to EWS how she felt but without any response. EWS provided a statement broadly agreeing with this account.

In December 2009, while EW was at an arranged appointment at the child development clinic in relation to ongoing problems related to his behaviour and development, a consultant paediatrician found significant bruising on the child's body, particularly in the area of his upper back. The children were removed from parental care and then returned to the family with the stipulation that the children and their parents reside with EWS's mother and her partner in order to provide supervision. This arrangement broke down in January 2010, largely due to the cramped living conditions in their two-bedroomed flat, since when the children have been in separate foster placements.

The nature of the injuries

The injuries to EW consisted of a number of discrete, linear marks on his upper back. These were consistent with bruising and were noted to run in a number of directions. There was an area of bruising noted on the left forearm and two linear parallel lines noted on his right anterior chest and shoulder area. Petechial bruising was noted on his right armpit and a small circular bruise in the inner aspect of his right upper arm. He also had bruising to both knees and shins.

Cause of injuries: mother's accounts

The mother told the doctor that she had been with the children and their father at an outdoor play area in December when EW and KW had been on the climbing frame and EW had fallen off it from a height. SM recalled that he had been very upset and that she had later looked at his back in the car but the marks did not appear until a day later. SM maintained this explanation for some time. In January 2010, SM made the following statement in which an entirely different version of the circumstances leading to the injuries was given:

I was awoken by [KW] and when I got up I realised that the children had been playing with water in the bathroom. [EW] had proceeded to soak his bedroom with cups of water and had taken the showerhead out of the shower in order to spray the landing, bathroom and stairs. He had also ripped wallpaper off the bedroom wall. At that point [EW] was on the top bunk bed in the room which he shares with [MW]. I ordered him to come down off the bed and he refused to do so. I accept that I lost my temper and that I grabbed him by the arm and pulled him across the bed to the steps of the bed. I did so by standing on the bottom bunk. I then pulled him down the steps of the bunk beds but as he was wearing a t-shirt he spiralled on the way down and hit the steps of the bunk beds. He then landed on the floor whilst I was still holding on to his t-shirt.

I have not put this explanation forward before now due to my terror that this momentary loss of control would result in my children being taken away from me for ever. We had been so happy to be back together as a family unit despite all of the challenges described above. I have been so upset since this incident and still find it hard to believe that the children have been returned to foster care.

Cause of injuries: the experts' view

Weir J had the benefit of assistance from respected experts in the fields of paediatrics, forensic pathology and forensic medicine, each of whom endeavoured to explain the possible aetiology of the marks seen on EW. However, none succeeded in doing so conclusively. As counsel for the parents pointed out, whatever problems had existed in this family that had caused social services to become and remain involved with them, there was no history of any physical abuse of any of the children by either parent at any time in the past. He also drew attention to the fact that there were a number of different theories as to how various of the injuries might have been caused, but the only one which might explain the pattern and distribution of all the injuries was that related to the bunk beds.

Conclusions

Acknowledging that the injuries were not accidentally sustained, Weir J stated the question as being whether it was more likely than not that they were not sustained in the course of the alleged bunk-bed incident. If they were not borne in that incident, then no other explanation than one of intentional infliction in some presently unknown manner seemed possible. The following list of factors, while not exhaustive, seemed to him to be of importance in assessing the likely truth of the matter:

'1. EW is and was a child given to particularly difficult behaviours which he exhibited not only when in the care of his mother but equally when in that of his foster carers and for which he was being seen at the child development clinic.

2. While at the family centre, SM had had advice and assistance in managing the three children together whereas following her move to the community she was dependent upon EWS, who had promised in advance that he would help and support her. By his own admission, the latter turned out to be a poor support indeed . . .

3. Given the low mental state into which SM had sunk by December 2009, when she discovered the havoc wreaked by the

children to their newly-decorated house and with EWS still sleeping soundly from a tiredness for which no energetic endeavour can have been responsible, it is not surprising that she lost her temper. Any parent might have struggled to contain theirs. Her account of the ensuing struggle with EW is entirely understandable though much to be regretted.

4. Is her account of the struggle sufficient to account for the injuries observed and photographed? . . . I conclude that the bunk-bed explanation, although it came late, is more likely than not to represent the true cause of these injuries. It follows that I am not satisfied that these injuries were intentionally inflicted by SM.'

Held
Injuries not deliberately inflicted.

Postscript
Weir J added the following postscript:

'The overall evidence in this case establishes that SM tried very hard to succeed, virtually single-handedly, in the particularly difficult task of parenting these children. I have no doubt that she loves them very much and that they love her. EWS was no real help to her nor in my estimation can he be counted on for the future. He was indeed a hindrance. SM needed what she did not have and, if the children return to her as I hope they will, will similarly for the future need namely, good, practical help. I am often struck in these cases by the paucity of such help for parents in the community, especially for parents who lack familial support. By comparison, the level of help and respite provided for foster carers seems for some reason to be very much greater . . . What is badly needed is more practical day-to-day support from people with practical parenting skills, probably more mature people who may have raised their own families and thereby learned from their own successes and mistakes. An investment in recruiting support of this type would be both effective and cost-effective in maintaining families within the community and avoiding the costly involvement of the care system . . . An outcome of permanent removal of children from their families is, too often, as much an indictment of a failed system as it is of inadequate parents.'

Comment
This is a rather odd finding in which Weir J would seem to have concluded that the child's injuries, though caused by the mother, were neither accidental nor deliberately inflicted. As he points out, the mother lost her temper in circumstances when many others might also do so. Arguably, this is just how many incidents of child harm, properly designated as NAI, occur.

However, there can be no quibbling with the good sense of his postscript. There does need to be a greater investment of state resources in situations of failing parenting in the brief window of opportunity before welfare interests dictate that the alternative, if draconian, option of permanency via adoption must be pursued. Residential assessment centres and social service facilities have their place, but programmes for parental skill development and empowerment are best delivered in the home setting where they need to be practised. Weir J is right to suggest that on-site mentoring by mature 'family aides', prepared to live in for periods when necessary, is more conducive to attaining 'good enough parenting' skills than relying solely on facility-based assessment and training, no matter how good the additional social work input.

The genetics of mental illness: a guide for parents and adoption professionals

Dr Rudolf Uher, Clinical Lecturer in Psychiatry at the MRC Social Genetic and Developmental Psychiatry Centre, Institute of Psychiatry, King's College London, prepared these notes

Mental illness in a family member can be a disturbing experience that is associated with high demands on carers and stigma. Therefore, it is understandable that people who are considering adoption request information about the likelihood that the child may develop mental illness, especially when one or both birth parents suffer from such a condition. It is the responsibility of adoption professionals to provide prospective parents with truthful and balanced information about the risk of mental illness in the child. In the rapidly evolving field of psychiatric genetics, finding the relevant information and interpreting it according to individual needs can prove challenging. The aim of this article is to summarise the relevant knowledge in an accessible manner.

How common is mental illness?

Before we think about the risk of mental illness in adopted individuals, it is useful to consider what mental illness is and how common it is in the general population. Many will be surprised to learn that mental illness is actually very common: approximately 30 in 100 individuals will experience symptoms that are sufficient for a diagnosis of at least one type of mental illness at some point in their lives. Most will have the more common forms of mental illness, such as anxiety or depression, which include experiences of low mood and fears known to everyone. These *common mental disorders*, whilst distressing and disabling, often get better with time or respond to adequate treatment. While anxiety and depression are more common in women, men are more prone to alcohol and substance addictions and antisocial behaviours, which are also classified as

mental illness, and can have massive impact on the individual and their family. Approximately three in 100 individuals in the general population will develop *severe mental illness*, such as schizophrenia or bipolar disorder. These conditions may present with episodes of extreme distress and visibly disturbed behaviour incomprehensible to others, require psychiatric hospital admissions and/or life-long treatment with medication, cause long-term disability and attract a disproportionate degree of stigma. Although the distinction between common mental disorders and severe mental illness is not entirely clear cut and there is significant variation of outcomes within each of these groups, it will be useful to consider them separately.

How much risk of mental illness is passed from parents to children?

It is an indisputable fact that mental illness runs in families. Having a close relative (eg parent) affected by mental illness puts one at a higher risk of developing mental illness. Studies of twins and adopted individuals show that most of the risk is carried by genes rather than family culture or environment. How high the risk is depends on whether one or both parents were affected and whether their illness is severe or not. The table overleaf helps estimate the risk of offspring developing mental illness that will require medical attention (see Dean *et al*, 2010; Gottesman *et al*, 2010).[1]

---

[1] These numbers are lower than for any mental disorder, since less than half of all people with mental illness seek medical help.

Health notes

Table 1

Estimating the risk of offspring developing mental illness that will require medical attention[2]

	Risk of any mental illness requiring medical attention (per 100 offspring)	Risk of severe mental illness (per 100 offspring)
Neither parent has mental illness	10	2
One parent has common mental disorder	20	4
One parent has severe mental illness	21	7
Both parents have common mental disorder	31	6
One parent has common and one has severe mental illness	33	11
Both parents have severe mental illness	36	32

Approximately ten in 100 individuals with two healthy parents will require treatment for a mental illness at some point. The risk doubles if one of the birth parents has mental illness and triples if both birth parents have mental illness. If the mental illness in birth parents is severe, the offspring are also more likely to suffer from severe mental illness. If both parents suffer from severe mental illness, the risk of severe mental illness in the offspring is approximately one in three. This varies slightly with the type of severe mental illness: offspring of two parents suffering from schizophrenia have a 39 in 100 risk of developing schizophrenia or similar illness in their life. Offspring of two parents with bipolar disorder have a 25 in 100 risk of bipolar disorder in addition to an eleven in 100 risk of depression. The risk is not entirely specific to one type of mental illness: for example, addiction in a parent not only increases the risk of addiction but also doubles the risk of schizophrenia in offspring. Therefore, asking about the risk of any mental

illness or severe mental illness makes more sense than asking about the risk of the exactly same disorder that has been diagnosed in a relative. In summary, the risk of mental illness is substantially elevated if both birth parents are affected. However, even with both birth parents suffering from severe mental illness, their children are still more likely to be healthy than ill (because all risks are less than 50 in 100).

Can we do anything to stop children at genetic risk from developing mental illness?

Perhaps the most interesting question is how so many people with high genetic risk loading remain healthy and resilient. Two important studies on adopted children of birth mothers with schizophrenia suggest that the key to ameliorating genetic risk lies in good parenting and stimulating environment during childhood and adolescence. A Finnish study followed adopted children of birth mothers with schizophrenia and looked at the interaction between the adoptive parents and children (Tienari *et al*, 2004). They found that the risk of schizophrenia was 36 in 100 among children brought up by adoptive parents who were somewhat critical, constrained or inconsistent in their communication with the children compared to only six in 100 among children brought up by adoptive parents who communicated clearly and consistently, without criticism and with clear boundaries. Importantly, all parents in the study were considered to be adequate and these levels of critical and constrained communication definitely did not 'cause' schizophrenia in children without genetic risk. However, very good and consistent parenting seems to reduce risk for schizophrenia among those at genetic risk. A large Swedish study found that risk of severe mental illness among adopted children of birth mothers with schizophrenia was more influenced by

---

[2] Table 1 is based on the Danish Population Registry 2010. Such data are not available in the UK. Since we have no reasons to believe that genetic risk differs between the UK and Denmark, these are the best estimates for the UK population as well.

the environment they were growing up in: it was increased if the adoptive parents were unemployed or were single parents and decreased in socioeconomically advantaged adoptive families with two employed parents (Wicks *et al*, 2010). These two important studies clearly show that genetic risk does not directly cause severe mental illness, but interacts with the environment. Consistent, resourceful and stimulating parenting in childhood can reduce the likelihood of developing mental illness in children at genetic risk.

Is there a genetic test?

With the recent advances in molecular genetics, it is tempting to imagine that genetic risk for mental illness can be directly measured by a genetic test and perhaps nullified by a targeted genetic intervention. The human genome contains 20 billion letters of the genetic alphabet (nucleotides) that compose the sequence of 20,000 genes and a lot of sequences in between the genes, the function of which is still little understood.

One human can differ from another in several million places of the genome (polymorphisms). It is now possible to measure more than one million polymorphisms at the same time and compare them between thousands of people with a disease and thousands of healthy controls. These massive experiments have churned out genetic variants that contribute to human disease, such as age-related blindness, dementias, diabetes and inflammatory bowel disease. With the impressive array of new genes for human disease, it is easy to overlook the fact that most of these links are very weak and contribute little to the prediction of risk for an individual. Moreover, genes predisposing to mental illness seem to be much more difficult to find. To date, only a handful of genetic variants have been identified, which appear likely to be associated with one type of mental illness or another. These gene-illness associations are weak and fragile. Scientists need many thousands of individuals to prove such associations

beyond reasonable doubt, and all put together, these genetic variants may only explain an exceedingly small fraction of the familial risk. This may be because the genes work in intricate interactions with the environment and with other genes or because each of the culprit genetic variants may be individually rare. The consequence is that there is no genetic test that could be used to predict the risk of mental illness in an individual and no such test is likely to appear in the near future.

In the absence of a genetic test, by far the best predictor of the risk of mental illness in an individual is whether their biological parents suffer from mental illness. Having a birth parent with schizophrenia increases one's risk of developing schizophrenia approximately ten times and this has been shown again and again in every population examined. In comparison, carrying a genetic variant identified as associated with schizophrenia will increase the risk less than 1.1 times, and this association often does not replicate in other populations. This does not stop commercial companies from offering genetic tests for the risk of mental illness to consumers who are willing to pay for these. Leaders in psychiatric genetics and professional bodies consider these practices as irresponsible and unethical, and regulatory agencies are preparing to ban the marketing of genetic testing directly to the consumer (Boddington, 2009; International Society of Psychiatric Genetics, 2009; Murray *et al*, 2010).

Conclusion

In conclusion, mental illness is partly heritable. Because parents with mental illness are sometimes as a consequence unable to take care of their children, relatively more children who are looked after and adopted carry genetic risk for mental illness. The degree of this risk can be estimated from medical histories of both birth parents. No genetic test is available that would add meaningful information. The genetic risk on its own does not determine the development of mental illness. Even children with both parents with severe mental illness are more likely to be healthy than ill. Resourceful parenting and supportive environment can modify the genetic risk substantially, but will not remove it completely. Prospective adoptive parents should receive balanced information to help them make decisions that are right for them and the children.

References

Boddington P, 'The ethics and regulation of direct-to-consumer genetic testing', *Genome Med* 1:7, p 71, 2009

Dean K, Stevens H, Mortensen PB, Murray RM, Walsh E and Pedersen CB, 'Full spectrum of psychiatric outcomes among offspring with parental history of mental disorder', *Arch Gen Psychiatry* 67:8, pp 822–29, 2010

Gottesman II, Laursen TM, Bertelsen A and Mortensen PB, 'Severe mental disorders in offspring with two psychiatrically ill parents', *Arch Gen Psychiatry* 67:3, pp 252–57, 2010

International Society of Psychiatric Genetics, 'Genetic testing for psychiatric disorders: a statement by the Board of Directors of the International Society of Psychiatric Genetics', 2009; available at www.ispg.net

Murray AB, Carson MJ, Morris CA and Beckwith J, 'Illusions of scientific legitimacy: misrepresented science in the direct-to-consumer genetic-testing marketplace', *Trends Genet*, 2010

Tienari P, Wynne LC, Sorri A, Lahti I, Laksy K, Moring J, Naarala M, Nieminen P and Wahlberg KE, 'Genotype-environment interaction in schizophrenia-spectrum disorder: long-term follow-up study of Finnish adoptees', *Br J Psychiatry* 184, pp 216–22, 2004

Wicks S, Hjern A and Dalman C, 'Social risk or genetic liability for psychosis? A study of children born in Sweden and reared by adoptive parents', *Am J Psychiatry* 167, pp 1240–46, 2010